A Nightmare in Villisca

Investigating the Haunted Axe Murder House

Also by Richard Estep

In Search of the Paranormal
Haunted Longmont
The World's Most Haunted Hospitals
The Farnsworth House Haunting
Trail of Terror
Colorado UFOs
The Devil's Coming to Get Me
The Fairfield Haunting
Haunted Healthcare
The Horrors of Fox Hollow Farm
Building the Write Life
The Hanging Pit
The Haunting of Asylum 49
Spirits of the Cage
The Black Monk of Pontefract

A Nightmare in Villisca

Investigating the Haunted Axe Murder House

Richard Estep

In memory of Darwin Linn,

Your legacy endures, sir.

Contents

Foreword

Introduction

1. Tragedy Strikes

2. "We Want Answers."

3. "Be Very Careful in this House."

4. "I Didn't do it to Myself."

5. Uninvited Guests

6. The Axe

7. Dedman's Hand

8. Playing Games

9. Asleep

10. Thought Form

11. A Glimpse of Hell

12. Houser Cards

13. "For Fun."

14. "The House Knows You're Coming."

15 Respect

16. Making sense of it All

Acknowledgments

Foreword

What can I possibly say that hasn't already been said about the Villisca Axe Murder House? My answer is: *plenty*.

My love for the paranormal started at a young age, with UFOs, and progressed to conspiracy theories, monsters, and mysteries. Ghosts were always kind of on my radar, but I didn't put much into researching them until my late teens.

As an adult, I have spent over 15 years running one of the most notorious and iconic houses in America: the Villisca Axe Murder House. I have done well over 400 overnights alone in the house, and compiled over fifteen years of data, from myself and from other well-respected teams, in order to look for patterns in the activity.

My thought was that surely, there had to be a repeating pattern of some kind. Why is there a lot of activity happening on some days, and on other days there is absolutely nothing at all? I have investigated the house during several of the anniversaries of the murder; on the birthdays of the victims; during storms, eclipses, you name it. What I have found so far is there is absolutely no known pattern to any of it.

In fact, the house seems to be constantly changing and

morphing, day by day. I can say that I have never had the same thing happen repeatedly, and in fact, each time I would investigate, it seemed like a whole new location, with responses that seemed to have nothing to do with what actually happened in the house.

At other times, it seemed as if the house was just toying with people. Could the house, in fact, be haunting *itself?* Could it be a doorway, where multiple spirits come and go as they please? Over the years, I have met and worked with some of the brightest and most innovative minds in the paranormal field, and I consider my friend and colleague Richard Estep to be near the top of the list. I'm honored to know him, and have worked beside him and trust his opinion on everything creepy...and it's a bonus that he's one of my favorite authors!

So, sit back, relax and dig into this book...because it's a good one!

Johnny Houser
Villisca, Iowa
August 2020

Introduction

We live during a time in which feelings of vulnerability are commonplace. One only has to switch on the TV, or surf one of the Internet's many questionable news sites for a short period of time, before a definite sense of anxiety and general unease sets in.

Headlines declare that the streets are no longer safe. Gun and knife crime are rampant. Road rage attacks are on the rise. People are getting beaten to within an inch of their lives in disputes with strangers over the most minor of complaints, such as not wearing a mask in Walmart.

Sometimes, it's easy to feel as if the world is on the brink of madness.

So, what do we do? We go home. Maybe we have a drink. Eat some comfort food. Binge something mindless on TV. Or perhaps, if we're being more constructive, we play with our children and express our love for our partner. Then, when the hour starts to get late, we go to our inner sanctum: our bedroom.

We brush our teeth, wash up, pull back the sheets, and climb into bed. Reach out a hand to switch off the light. Plump up the pillows and then curl up under the covers. All being well, sleep takes us before too long. We drift off into peaceful slumber, hopefully to dream happy dreams, and temporarily escape from the chaos and the lunacy, before the arrival of morning brings it all crashing back down on us again.

We enjoy our greatest peace while we're at rest. Our parasympathetic nervous system, known informally to medical professionals the world over as the "rest and digest" system, is in charge. Our heart rate slows down. Our breathing pattern deepens, and also slows. The brain slips into a completely different mode of operation.

The very last thing we're expecting is danger, and quite rightly so. We're at home, with the doors and windows locked, lying safe in our beds; the safest, most protected place in the whole world.

Until it isn't.

There is something deeply visceral about the idea of a houseful of slumbering people, blissfully unaware that anything was wrong, being brutally killed in their beds. It strikes down the notion that we truly are safe in that most private of places, the bedroom, and during that most vulnerable of mental states: sleeping.

Perhaps this explains the American public's enduring

fascination with the infamous Villisca Axe Murders, as the events of June 9/10, 1912, are better known. Enter the name of Villisca, Iowa, into an Internet search engine, and the top results all link to that same dreadful night.

The United States has seen many murders that were more brutal, but few that touch us at our core, as those which took place in Villisca do. The loss of an entire family, including six innocent children, over the course of one night is the stuff of which tragedy is made. The stories claiming that the house is now haunted, which have circulated ever since the restoration of the property in the 1990s, have only served to add yet another dimension to an already curious and fascinating tale.

Back in 2017, I was staying at Malvern Manor, conducting a paranormal investigation over the space of several days that would form the basis for my book *The Devil's Coming to Get Me: The Haunting of Malvern Manor*. During that time, a voice came through our spirit box that said the word *Houser*. Of course, that could only mean one thing: the man himself, Johnny Houser. Johnny had spent a lot of time investigating at Malvern Manor himself, even going on to record a TV show for the VidiSpace platform called *Johnny Houser versus Malvern*

Manor, and although he sadly wasn't able to come over and investigate the Manor with us in person, I thought that it might be helpful if we got him to phone in. I was fascinated with the idea that the Villisca Axe Murderer may have stayed at Malvern Manor either before or after committing the heinous crime.

It was early in the evening when Johnny picked up the phone. He was sitting on the couch in the downstairs parlor of the Axe Murder House, and had a few minutes free to talk with us before turning the keys over to the people who had rented the place that night.

"I've got some time to kill before they get here," Johnny said, unknowingly winning the award for the least tasteful choice of phrasing imaginable. "Want me to see if I can stir something up for you guys?"

Did we *ever*.

Our small group of investigators went over to the so-called Shadow Man Hallway, at the far end of the Manor, and I set my phone down in the middle of the floor. Johnny had already run into the infamous Shadow Man in person. It had been part human-shaped shadow figure, part amorphous black mass. The thing took a run at him, as it has with several other visitors, before disappearing right in front of his face.

"It was freaky, scary, and downright odd," Johnny recalled, talking to us over the speakerphone. "I felt like this thing somehow *knew* me."

But what about there being a possible Malvern/Villisca connection?

"The newspapers at the time actually said that the Devil got off the train in Villisca that night," he went on. "Which is pretty darn creepy, when you stop to think about it."

I couldn't have agreed with him more. He added that when he encountered the Shadow Man, he developed an immediate sense of familiarity — becoming convinced that the entity, whatever it was, somehow knew him. I speculated that perhaps it had been over at the Villisca Axe Murder House at some point, because a number of visitors at that location had reported encountering something similar.

"So, spirits of Malvern Manor...this is Johnny Houser. I've got some friends that are staying there tonight. They'd love to communicate with you. Now, you know me. You ran right at me."

From a little further behind us along the empty hallway, there came a loud knock.

"If you have something to do with Villisca, well, I'm

sitting here at the Villisca Axe Murder House right now. Were you a living being at one point in time, or are you some sort of entity that never was human, that never lived a physical life? We just want to know who you are and what you are."

After spending a few more minutes in the Shadow Man Hallway, we then relocated up to the second floor, to a place known as Hank's Room. This was where the Spirit Box had spoken Johnny's name, so it seemed like a safe bet. I set the phone down carefully on top of a dresser which still contained a few of Hank's old clothes, musty but neatly-folded.

"Hank, buddy, what's going on?" Johnny called out. "My friends there tell me that you were talking about me earlier tonight. What is it that you want? What can I do for you?" There was no response. Johnny continued, "What I really want to know, Hank, is this...is there a link between Malvern Manor and the Villisca Axe Murder House? Because I'm sitting in that house right now, and — *WOW!*"

There was a long pause. When he returned, Johnny explain that he had just heard a series of loud knocks coming from up above him, on the second floor of the house. He had gone up there to check it out. Of course, nobody was there.

He was the only living person in the house that night.

Right there and then, I knew that I wanted to investigate the Villisca Axe Murder House, and try to unravel its story for myself. The book that you are now reading is my attempt to do just that.

Please note that this is not meant to be a definitive retelling of the murders themselves. Readers that would like complete details of the crime are referred to three excellent books: *Villisca,* by Roy Marshall; *Murdered in Their Beds,* by Troy Taylor; and *The Man from The Train*, by Bill James and Rachel McCarthy James. When studied together, these books provide an excellent overview of the Villisca Axe Murders, and helps set them in place within a much broader context.

I am now done with the Villisca Axe Murder House, having just returned from my fourth and final research trip. It has been a wild and crazy adventure, one which saw me take up residence inside the house for several days and nights, and I wouldn't have missed it for the world.

There's a story to be told.

Shall we go?

CHAPTER ONE
Tragedy Strikes

According to Tom Savage, author of the book *A Dictionary of Iowa Place-Names* (University of Iowa Press, 2007) the railroad town of Villisca was given its name because of its similarity to the Native American word, *Waliska*. They believed that the word meant "pretty view" or "pleasant place."

This is, unfortunately, incorrect.

Waliska actually means "evil spirit." This seems particularly apropos to our story, which began in the long, hot summer of 1912, and continues on to the present day.

April 15, 1912 — the sea-going liner RMS TITANIC sinks in the frigid waters of the Atlantic Ocean. It will dominate the front-page newspaper headlines all across the United States...until the tragedy is supplanted by another, which takes place on the night of Sunday, June 9 and the early morning hours of Monday, June 10.

In its aftermath, the small town of Villisca would never be the same again.

Josiah Moore, aged 43, made a living in the hardware business, helping keep the local farmers supplied with the items that were necessary for them to make a living. His wife, Sara Moore (formerly Montgomery), age 40, kept house and took care of their four children: Herman, age 11; Katherine, age 10; Arthur Boyd, age 7; and Paul, age 5.

In Villisca, Sunday meant one thing: getting ready to go to church. Along with the rest of the country, most Iowans went to church religiously (if you'll pardon the pun) on the Sabbath. The Moores were no exception, attending the Presbyterian church that was – and still is – located just a short distance away from their comfortable but modest home. This was to be an evening service, a special event held on behalf of the children.

Katherine Moore met two of her friends at the service that day, Lena, age 11, and Ina Stillinger, age 8, the daughters of farmer Joe Stillinger and his wife. The Stillingers lived on the very outskirts of town. Joe was not overly fond of attending church, nor of his daughters going by themselves, but they were nevertheless allowed to go on the evening of June 9. There was no way that their parents could have foreseen the tragic outcome of that decision.

Children love to have sleepovers, and between them, the three girls decided that the Stillinger sisters should spend the night at the Moore house with their friend Katherine. Josiah and Sara were inclined to indulge their daughter, and after a phone call was placed to the Stillinger farm, they were granted permission to stay.

Much fun must have been had at the church, and although the precise time isn't known, it is estimated that the Moores and their two houseguests wouldn't return home until somewhere between 9:30 and 10:30 that night.

It's doubtful that there were signs of anything being obviously amiss at the Moore House, and if there was, no evidence has survived to tell us about it. In terms of the specific sequence of events, much of what happens next is informed conjecture, rather than hard, proven fact. Highly-qualified and experienced homicide detectives and criminal profilers have examined the case in minute detail, and given their educated opinions, but at the end of the day, the state of the crime scene itself can only tell us so much.

For one thing, there are competing theories as to how the murderer entered the home. Some students of the case believe that the killer broke into the house while the Moores were at the Presbyterian Church, skulking in the attic, or even hiding in the closet in the children's bedroom upstairs on the second floor. He would then have waited until the lights were out before embarking on a killing spree. The obvious drawback to this theory is that the murderer would have risked detection by Josiah or Sara Moore as they went about the business of closing up the house and putting the children to bed, which meant they would have been less vulnerable and far more likely to fight back.

Another theory counters with the prospect that the killer didn't enter the Moore house until much later that night, when all of the occupants were fast asleep. An adult-sized depression in the bed of hay inside the barn implied that the killer may have lain there during the daytime, covertly watching the comings and goings surrounding the Moore house and those of its neighbors through a hole in the wall. Waiting patiently in the manner of a hunter stalking his prey, he could have assessed the number and physical characteristics of his potential victims, noting that there was only one adult male for him to overcome if things did not go according to plan.

The murderer took Josiah Moore's own axe, presumably from outside the house or inside the barn. This was later confirmed by Josiah's brother, Charles, who inspected the implement carefully and recognized a specific defect on the axe blade. It hadn't been particularly well cared for, being more blunt than sharp and containing a fair amount of rust.

Whether he was lurking inside the house already, or had to make entry through a downstairs window or door, the killer dealt with the two greatest potential threats first: Josiah and Sara Moore. Both were killed in their bed, located in the master bedroom at the top of the staircase. The axe was swung with such force that its head grazed the ceiling, leaving a series of telltale gouges. The Moores both lay on their backs, the mattress and pillows beneath their heads saturated with blood. Sara and Josiah Moore had both been struck repeatedly with the axe, their faces rendered almost completely unrecognizable in the savage assault. Worse still, their children were all also battered to death, each of them being killed with the flat of the axe head.

Although we will never know for sure, it is believed that the four Moore children were killed next, as all of them lay sleeping in their beds in the south-facing upstairs bedroom. This ceiling also bore several marks that were suggestive of an axe's backswing, and future tenants of the house would go on to claim that a number of faded brown splatter stains were still visible on the walls many years after the murders took place.

The murderer then went downstairs and killed Ina and Lena Stillinger. Satisfied that everybody in the house was now dead, he set about making sure that he would not be disturbed for the next few hours. Closing all of the curtains to shut out any prying eyes, he also covered the large mirror on the dresser with one of Sara Moore's skirts — perhaps because some part of him was disgusted by the repugnant act that he had just carried out. It may be that in his state of self-loathing, he did not want to accidentally catch sight of himself while covered in the blood of innocents.

With the house completely blacked out, he used kerosene lamps rather than candles in order to find his way around. In order to either kill, or cope with the emotional response to killing fellow human beings, particularly children, it becomes necessary for some murderers to depersonalize their victims. One of the most effective ways to do that is to cover up their faces. (This technique, incidentally, is also used today in the field of medical education – in human cadaver dissection labs, instructors will typically cover the cadaver's face until the very end of the class, in order to prevent the students from making an emotional connection with the subject that they are cutting up).

By this same token, the killer then moved from body to body, carefully drawing a bedsheet over each one, completely covering the head. Other items of clothing that he found inside the house were draped over their faces. In his mind, perhaps, this would have prevented them from judging him with their eyes, serving to turn them from flesh and blood human beings into inanimate objects.

Lena Stillinger was singled out for one final, gut-wrenching indignity. Her underwear was removed, after which she was deliberately positioned in such a way as to draw attention to her nudity, with both legs splayed. The killer then used a large cut of bacon wrapped in linen to masturbate with, most likely while he was standing over the poor girl's dead body. When he was finished, he dropped the bacon on the floor of the downstairs bedroom. It would be found there later that same day.

He then took some time to wash and clean himself up before leaving the house, closing the door and locking it behind him with a key that had been left in the lock by Mr. or Mrs. Moore.

Nobody saw him leave.

The Moore house sat silently until daybreak.

The Moores were usually up and about early in the morning, having a number of animals in their yard whose needs must be taken care of. It was most unlike them to sleep in, especially on a weekday, and one of their neighbors found it rather peculiar when she hadn't seen Josiah taking care of his chores that Monday morning. The house itself showed no signs of life. With the drapes drawn, an eerie stillness had seemed to settle over the place.

Finally, the neighbor, a Mrs. Mary Peckham, grew concerned enough to approach the house and knock on the door. There was no answer. She knew the Moores well enough to feel comfortable with going inside, but the doors to the house were all locked.

Josiah's brother, Ross Moore, finally arrived with a key. He was the first to enter the house. Call it intuition, or call it gut instinct, but he could tell straight away that something was wrong. His suspicions were confirmed when he went into the downstairs bedroom and, despite the gloom, his eyes could make out two unmoving forms lying on the bed, completely covered up with bedding but unmistakably dead. There was blood splattered all around them.

Unwilling to go any further, Ross immediately left the house and sent for the marshal, Hank Horton. A more in-depth search of the house subsequently confirmed their worst fears: everybody inside the Moore residence was dead, most likely killed by the axe which was found resting casually against one of the walls. Upstairs, the bedroom walls were also stained with arterial blood. It had come from the heads of the six victims, each of whom had sustained what medical professionals today refer to as "injuries incompatible with life."

In other words, the blunt force head trauma was so severe, the victims' skulls had been completely shattered, their faces distorted and stove in. A number of those who witnessed the grisly sight, even medical men of many years' experience, were haunted by it for the rest of their lives.

Incredibly, the idea of preserving the crime scene in order to prevent the contamination of evidence didn't seem to cross anybody's mind. A constant stream of interested parties paraded through the Moore House on the morning of June 10, including a number of doctors. Based upon the degree of rigor mortis and dependent lividity — the tendency of blood to pool in the lowest part of the body after the heart has stopped beating — the doctors believed that the murders had taken place at or around midnight the previous evening.

Showing absolutely no sense of shame or respect, various members of the public managed to finagle their way inside, ghoulishly eager to see the grisly murder scene with their own eyes. When the coroner arrived at nine o'clock, he had to push his way through a jostling crowd of people that had gathered in front of the house. They defied all efforts to control them or to keep them out. By the time this stampede of locals had finally abated somewhat, dispersed by the arrival of more law enforcement officers, irreparable damage had been done to the integrity of the crime scene. In order to protect what little remained, it was necessary for the police to string loops of barbed wire around the perimeter of the Moore House.

Yet the tourists kept on coming, from all over Villisca and the areas surrounding it. Everybody wanted to experience the gruesome spectacle for themselves, and some didn't want to take no for an answer. Journalists came next, drawn by what they knew would make a spectacular headline story.

Once their curiosity was satisfied, and the full extent of the violence inflicted upon the Moores and the Stillinger children began to sink in, the mood of the townsfolk started to turn ugly. Just what kind of monster could have done something like this, they wanted to know, and where exactly could this beast be hiding?

One thing was for sure — he couldn't have gotten too far. Perhaps he was still within the town itself, keeping a low profile and getting ready to strike again once the people of Villisca went to bed later that night. The very thought of it both terrified and enraged them in equal measure. The men of the town formed into mobs, arming themselves and setting out to track down every stranger in town. All it took was the merest rumor of an unfamiliar person seen walking along the road outside of town to send a gaggle of angry Villisca men in pursuit.

Meanwhile, the town itself was turned upside down in a search for the killer's hiding place that left no stone unturned. Pet dogs were pressed into service as makeshift bloodhounds. Barns, outhouses, alleyways, even thickets and stands of trees...all were checked, and checked again, in an attempt to uncover the location of the Villisca Axe Man.

He was never found.

When genuine bloodhounds, well-trained and with extensive experience in tracking down suspects, were brought to Villisca, the citizens grew optimistic that the culprit would finally be caught. The hounds and their handler arrived as quickly as the train service would allow. Starting at the crime scene, they were allowed to sniff the murder weapon itself in order to familiarize themselves with the killer's spoor, and were then turned loose.

A ripple of excitement went through the crowd when the bloodhounds swiftly picked up a trail, and began to follow it through the streets of Villisca. Sweeping along behind them came the townsfolk, each of them wanting to be there when the monster was finally caught. No doubt they were in the mood for a lynching.

The hounds stopped momentarily at the mansion of Frank Jones, who would go on to be named as one of the prime suspects in the case, before following the invisible trail toward the outskirts of town.

The farther the bloodhounds went, the more excited people became. Nothing had united the people of Villisca quite like this ever before, and nothing ever would again. They all shared the same desire: to see the man who had butchered eight of their neighbors pay for his crimes with his life.

Their hopes were dashed when the trail suddenly dead-ended at the banks of the river. The dogs stopped, panting. Their work was done, and they could go no further.

Back in Villisca, the bodies of the eight victims would be taken to the local firehouse, where the morticians did their very best to make them presentable. It cannot have been an easy job, even for the most professional of morticians, because the wounds inflicted upon each of the victims' heads were so grievous. There is only so much that even the most skilled of undertakers can do in the face of such damage.

Thousands of mourners had come from miles around to see the murder victims laid to rest. They lined up to pay their respects to the Moore Family and the Stillinger girls on the day of their funeral, June 12. At the request of Mayor F.L. Ingman, all of the town's businesses shut their doors for the afternoon. At the Villisca firehouse, the caskets had been placed side by side, all in a row. The firehouse bay doors were opened, allowing the people of the town to walk through and offer their final condolences to their murdered neighbors.

One cannot help but imagine that in each of their minds, the same thought must have been churning round and round: *That could have been my family. That could have been *us*.*

Services were held in the park, as the cemetery could not

possibly accommodate such a throng of people. Horse-drawn hearses and wagons then conveyed the eight coffins from the firehouse to their final resting place in the town cemetery.

Although the science of forensics was still in its infancy, efforts were made to fingerprint the crime scene — but to no avail. Analysis suggested that the killer was either left-handed, or at the very least, had utilized the axe in the manner of a man who was left hand dominant. Beyond that, little else could be gleaned.

With the prospect of justice now slipping through their fingers, the people of Villisca felt their righteous anger give way to something else: fear.

The killer was still out there, his identity as yet unknown. Despite the extensive searches that they had made, and the best efforts of the bloodhounds, he appeared to have literally gotten away with murder. Who was to say that this maniac wouldn't chance his hand again? Worse, what if the killer was one of *them,* living in their midst, participating in the searches himself, and all the while laughing inwardly at their failure to uncover him?

A blanket of panic descended upon Villisca. Sales of locks and reinforcing hardware skyrocketed. Neighbors took to doubling up, sleeping together in one house so that the male heads of each family could stand watch at night, alternating with one another. The men of Villisca burned the midnight oil for weeks after the murders, staying awake through the night with a shotgun or a rifle sitting in their lap, just waiting for the sound of somebody trying to force entry into their homes.

Crude alarms were fashioned, tripwires strung across porches and doorframes that hooked into tin cans, so that any killer creeping up in the night would cause them to rattle...and find themselves on the receiving end of both barrels of a shotgun.

With hindsight, it's remarkable that more people weren't accidentally killed, the victims of an itchy trigger finger.

The list of potential suspects was initially rather broad. If you had been seen within twenty-five miles of the town around the time of the murders, and nobody local knew who you were, or nobody was willing to vouch for you, then you were a suspect. It was as simple as that.

A small group of homeless men — *hoboes,* in the parlance of the time — had been camped on the outskirts of Villisca for a while. Most of them were African-Americans, which only made them seem more suspicious in the eyes of the white population. Once news of the murders reached them, they broke camp and put as much distance between themselves and Villisca as possible, wisely hopping on a train and heading for the hills before the finger of blame was pointed squarely at them.

Villisca had started out its life as a railroad town, and as such, a lot of people rode the trains through there, getting on and off whenever they felt like it. A number of these travelers were transients, simply passing through on their way from one rail stop to another, drifting aimlessly from town to town. One commonly-held theory concerning the identity of the murderer is that he was just such a person, and that the axe murders, rather than being premeditated and meticulously planned, were nothing more than a random crime of opportunity, committed by a traveling psychopath who was riding the railroad, killing whenever the mood struck him.

As the days passed, slowly turning into weeks, then months, and finally years, those law enforcement officers who pursued the case grew no closer to definitively identifying their suspect. Any danger there may have been that the cold case would be dismissed and forgotten was averted by the Moore and Stillinger families, both of whom worked tirelessly to demand answers and to keep the hunt for their loved ones' killer moving forward.

Arguably the most prominent suspect was Iowa State Senator Frank Jones. A self-made man, Jones's power and influence were said to be matched only by his arrogance. He was not well-liked by those who knew him, regarded by many as being pompous and self-centered.

Jones' connection with J.B. Moore was plain to see. He had been Josiah's employer several years before his murder. The two had parted ways after almost ten years, and the separation had been quite acrimonious. To add insult to injury in Jones' eyes, his former employee had the nerve to start his own rival business right there in Villisca, acting in direct competition to his own interests. Undoubtedly there was no love lost between the two men, who wouldn't even exchange a polite greeting whenever they ran into one another in public.

Nevertheless, was a professional rivalry enough to drive Frank Jones to commit — or as the rumors held, pay to have a proxy commit — the brutal murder of not just his rival, but also the man's entire family and two unrelated children? I consider that to be unlikely, but the bad blood between Jones and J.B. Moore went deeper than that. Jones' son Albert had married a lady named Dona, and it wasn't long before rumors began to circulate that Dona and J.B. Moore were engaged in an illicit love affair.

Dona Jones had acquired a reputation for having an inappropriate number of "gentlemen callers," usually when her husband was away. One of those callers was said to have been Josiah Moore.

Whether there was truth to these rumors or not is almost irrelevant. This was the early 20th century, after all, and many societal customs and mores were Victorian in nature. "Face" was everything, and for a man as powerful as Frank Jones, a politician who moved in highly influential circles, the stories of an affair must have been seen as a very public form of humiliation.

Because of this, it was proposed by representatives of a private detective agency that Jones Junior and Senior had paid one William "Blackie" Mansfield to commit the murders on his behalf. Mansfield was a convicted criminal with an unsavory reputation. In a macabre turn of events, his own family were murdered with an axe by an unknown assailant just two years after the Villisca Axe Murders took place.

There was just one problem: William Mansfield had an alibi for June 9 and 10, in the form of several signed and witnessed payroll documents from a railroad job he had been working at the time. Therefore, it was argued, he could not have been present in Villisca when the Moores were killed. Although aspersions would be cast on this alibi, Mansfield walked free in 1916 when the case was brought before the Grand Jury.

In this author's opinion, one of the bigger flaws in the theory that Frank Jones was behind the Villisca Axe Murders is that he had such a great deal to lose. Setting his other alleged faults aside, Jones was a shrewd and canny businessman, attributes which also served him well in the political arena. He had to have known that if his involvement in such a horrific and repugnant crime was to be uncovered, then everything he had worked so hard to achieve — power, prestige, and a lofty social position — would disappear in a puff of smoke, his name and reputation irretrievably tarnished. Not to mention the small matter of spending the rest of his life in prison, or possibly even being sentenced to death.

Yes, Frank Jones hated Josiah Moore...but did he hate him enough to risk everything, up to and including his own life, in order to lash out at him and even the score?

Personally, I doubt it.

The matter did not end with Mansfield's acquittal, however. More rumors began to circulate, this time alleging that Frank Jones had rigged the jury in order to get the defendant off Scot Free. Presumably this was done to prevent Mansfield from implicating his employer, in order to get a reduced sentence.

The private detective who had led the charge against William Mansfield, one James Wilkerson, began holding public meetings in and around Villisca. He alleged that not only was Mansfield guilty of the murders, but that he had evidence to prove that he had been acting on the direct orders of Frank Jones. Public sentiment began to turn against Jones, who, seeing his political career being threatened, responded by lodging a law suit for slander against Wilkerson.

The subsequent trial was something of a circus, with a packed courtroom hanging on every word of both the defense and the prosecution. Public interest only intensified when the focus of the trial switched from addressing the question of whether James Wilkerson had slandered Frank Jones, to the accusation that Frank Jones really *had* been the driving force behind the Villisca Axe Murders. It was a brilliant move on the part of Wilkerson's lawyer, an act of legal misdirection that one has to admire, even if it is difficult to condone.

The defense produced several witnesses, all of whom told stories that incriminated Frank Jones in the murders. In the words of one supposed eyewitness, William Mansfield was placed outside the Moore home the week of June 2, in the company of two other men. The same witness testified under oath that she had then seen the men meet with Frank Jones, who she claimed to have heard say, "Hit Joe first, and the rest will be easy."

Things were not looking good for Frank Jones. They took a turn for the worse when another witness stated that he had seen Albert Jones entering the Moore House on the night of June 9, while Josiah and his family were out attending church.

Despite the best efforts of Jones' attorney, and the fact that some of the eyewitness testimony had been questionable, to say the least, the jury finally returned a verdict that favored the defendant. This meant that not only was James Wilkerson found not guilty of slandering Frank Jones, but that by implication, Jones could quite possibly be guilty of the Villisca Axe Murders.

It was nothing short of a bombshell for Frank Jones, who

had gone into the slander trial with the full expectation of restoring his tarnished reputation, only to see it dragged even further through the mud, and find himself accused of something far worse. His once-stellar political career would soon wind up in tatters.

If only there happened to be another potential suspect, somebody that fit the bill as the Villisca killer far better than William Mansfield ever had.

A man like Reverend George Kelly.

By all accounts, Reverend George Kelly was a strange and troubled man. Some went so far as to call him "crazy" and "disturbed."

British by birth, Kelly lived in the town of Macedonia, some 40 miles from Villisca. Unlike William Mansfield, he was undeniably present in Villisca on the night of the murders. He also made a suspiciously fast getaway the following morning, at a time when everybody else in the vicinity was clamoring to get into the Moore House.

With Mansfield now out of the frame, Kelly was looking like a good candidate to be the Villisca Axe Murderer.

According to several contemporary accounts, Kelly's affect went beyond mere eccentricity or oddness. He was sometimes known to scare people simply by being in their presence, raising subliminal red flags of the kind that are ignored at one's peril. In modern-day parlance, he might be termed a "creeper."

Not only is Kelly known to have been in Villisca on June 9, but he was also sighted at the same Presbyterian church that the Moore family were attending that evening. One cannot help but wonder whether his eye was drawn to the Stillinger girls and their friends, the Moore children, particularly young Katherine Moore. The very thought of it is enough to make one shudder.

Roy Marshall, authority on the Villisca Axe Murders and author of the book *Villisca*, firmly believes that Kelly is the guilty party. I won't say that I disagree with him, because I do think that Kelly is a solid suspect – up to a point – but there are a number of things that don't quite add up about the behavior of this warped holy man. He is one of the most curious, controversial, and fascinating figures involved with the entire Villisca case.

For starters, one would expect somebody who was guilty of murdering a whole family in the night to quietly slip out of town (which he did) and to keep a low profile (which he most certainly did not). In fact, rather than fly under the radar, Reverend Kelly did the very opposite, bombarding the mailboxes of numerous officials and interested parties in the case with letters in which he described various prurient details concerning the murders. This quite understandably rang alarm bells, and helped put Kelly under a very unflattering spotlight.

The only thing that led to Kelly being dismissed as a suspect during the initial investigation in the summer of 1912, was his reputation for mental instability. The man was quite obviously mad, detectives reasoned, and therefore not only was he probably subject to deluded flights of fantasy where the murders were concerned, but he was unlikely to be found competent to stand trial anyway.

Two years later, Kelly was caught sending letters soliciting an underage girl into taking off her clothes for him, and also into performing sexual favors. Yet rather than go to jail for these offenses, he was instead institutionalized after being declared insane. Upon his release, the good reverend was far from cured. He acquired a well-deserved reputation for being a Peeping Tom, narrowly evading a beating from angry husbands for looking into windows as their wives were getting undressed.

As Kelly began to appear increasingly unhinged, detectives started to dig a little more deeply into his connection with the Moore family murders. What they found was damning. He had been seen laundering a blood-stained shirt in the days after the killings. Two eyewitnesses recalled encountering him on the train departing from Villisca early on the morning of June 10. After falling into conversation with this odd Englishman, the topic soon turned to the brutal axe murders which had just taken place in the town the night before. The truly strange thing was that word of the murders should not have gotten out yet. It wasn't to become public news until later that day. How, then, could Kelly have known about them, unless he had been involved somehow?

George Kelly was arrested and charged with murder in 1917...on just one single count, that of Lena Stillinger.

During his term of imprisonment while awaiting trial, the authorities had the opportunity to observe Kelly as he chopped wood in the jail yard. He demonstrated a distinctly left-handed bias with the axe, just as the Villisca Axe Murderer was believed to have done.

After having been placed in a cell with two undercover operatives posing as inmates, Kelly was cajoled into confessing to the Villisca murders during a marathon overnight interrogation session that was more about forcing him to own up to the crime than ascertaining the truth. "Coerced" is too weak a word for what happened to George Kelly. The man was almost certainly browbeaten and intimidated into confessing. He was most likely roughed up physically during the process.

Whether he was telling the truth or not is something that students of the case still debate passionately to this day.

Did Kelly have the means, the motive, and the opportunity to have done so? He was certainly physically capable of taking an axe and swinging it multiple times. His log-splitting in the jail yard had proven that. Although he was short in stature, Kelly was a wiry man and did not lack for strength.

As far as the motive is concerned, his well-documented sexual perversion and liking for vulnerable young girls seem like reason enough for him to have committed the crime of molesting Lena Stillinger. There was no way he could have done so and then allowed the other occupants of the house to live and bear witness to this vile act.

Lastly, we come to the opportunity. While in Villisca, Kelly was staying in the home of another man of the cloth who, due to a respiratory condition, happened to be sleeping outdoors in a tent in order to get some fresh air and alleviate the symptoms. This meant that Kelly could have snuck out of the house and committed the murders without his absence ever having been noticed.

The means, the motive, and the opportunity were all there.

On the face of it, Kelly's confession seems like a slam-dunk. He described hearing voices and noises in his head which compelled him to leave the house and go out for an evening walk. Lost in a mental fog, he suddenly found himself standing outside the house of Josiah Moore and his family.

"I felt God wanted me to slay utterly," he said to his interrogator. In other words, the voice of God had made him do it. Reverend George Kelly was not the first accused person to employ that defense, and he was certainly not the last. Taking J.B. Moore's own axe, he entered the house and bypassed the downstairs bedroom in which Ina and Lena Stillinger slept. His first stop was the master bedroom, Kelly claimed, killing Josiah with the axe, then turning his attention to the man's wife.

Their four children were murdered next in the south

bedroom. God continued to talk to him, urging him to keep on killing. Going back downstairs, he said that he had murdered Ina and Lena last.

Yet James Wilkerson, along with many of the townsfolk of Villisca, would not buy into Reverend Kelly being the murderer. The issue was fractious, splitting the opinion of the local residents and creating an acrimonious divide between those who thought Kelly had killed the Moores, and the Wilkerson-driven theory that William Mansfield was the guilty man, albeit at the behest of Frank Jones.

Nevertheless, Kelly had been charged and was duly tried in court. His lawyer was excellent, meticulously casting doubt on and poking holes in the key points being made by the prosecution. Now that push had come to shove, the witnesses who had claimed to have spoken with Kelly on the train on the morning of June 10 were suddenly doubtful about the date of their journey.

It had started out as a seemingly open and shut case. Now, reasonable doubt had begun to creep in. In a court of law, reasonable doubt is all that is needed to acquit. The prosecution's case was crumbling right in front of their eyes. At the end of the trial, eleven members of the jury were in agreement: they wanted to acquit Kelly. The twelfth just couldn't agree, thinking that he was guilty, but not responsible due to his being criminally insane. No matter what, Juror Number Twelve just would not budge, thereby creating a hung jury.

There was no other option. Reverend George Kelly would have to be tried again, by a completely different jury. This time, he was acquitted. He wasted no time in putting not just Villisca, but also the State of Iowa behind him. Now, perhaps finally having learned his lesson, he was wise enough to disappear into obscurity.

Many find George Kelly to be a very credible suspect in the case, and it is entirely possible that they are right. There are also those who feel the same way about Frank Jones, which I believe is a much greater stretch. But what of other potential candidates?

Another name that frequently rears its head in relation to the Villisca Axe Murders is that of Henry Lee Moore. Although it is the most famous case of its kind, many people are unaware that the Villisca Axe Murders are but one of several similar crimes which took place throughout the region; they have become collectively known as the Midwest Axe Murders.

At first glance, 35-year-old Henry Moore looks to be an appropriate suspect, not least because of a conviction he would sustain for murdering two women with an axe — his mother and grandmother, both of whom died while they slept. Yet there is no evidence placing Moore (who was not related to the dead family) in Villisca on or around the date of June 9/10. He ultimately did serve hard time for murdering two of his own family members (his mother and grandmother) with an axe, but never stood trial for the Villisca Axe Murders. Had he done so, the lack of anything other than circumstantial evidence would have made him a very tough sell to any jury that was assigned to hear the case.

Lastly, we come to one of the more intriguing candidates for the Villisca Axe Murderer: the so-called "Man from the Train." This idea, put forward by authors Bill James and Rachel McCarthy James in their book of the same name, holds that a former farmhand and manual laborer named Paul Mueller was responsible for a string of murders carried out over a period of many years. The murders spanned multiple communities, states, and even decades.

James and James make a compelling case for this

itinerant hobo having broken into the Moore House that night and killing everybody he found within, driven by sexual lusts that he could not control. For those seeking a fresh perspective on the Villisca Axe Murders, and their possible place in a bigger picture, *The Man from The Train* is well worth reading.

Only one thing is truly certain: the debate as to the killer's identity is never going away. So long has passed, and so much evidence has been obscured or lost (much in the immediate aftermath of the crime) that the murderer has almost certainly gotten away Scot Free.

Yet, after-echoes of the tragedy still remain, and it is those that we shall confront during the course of this book.

Ownership of the Moore House passed through several sets of hands over the years, and more than a few renters took up residence there. Finally, in 1994, came some stability, when the house was purchased by Darwin and Martha Linn. There had been few, if any, claims of paranormal activity surrounding the place before then (at least, not as far as the Linns were aware) and they had purchased it purely for its historical value. Darwin and Martha weren't trying to pick up a property, flip it, and make a quick buck. They saw that the house had a vitally important place in the history of not just Villisca, but also of the entire United States. To allow it to have simply fallen into disrepair and then ruin would have been a great shame.

Darwin and Martha knew that a lot of time, effort, and money needed to be put into restoring the house, and it was a commitment from which they did not shirk. When asked by former detective Steve DiSchiavi whether she thought that the regular visits of paranormal enthusiasts and groups were stirring up activity in the house, Martha said that many of those visitors had told her the phenomena started after the restoration was completed. It was the act of restoring the Moore House to some semblance of its old self that had triggered the perpetual stream of paranormal activity that is still experienced to this day.

I suspect that she may be on to something there. It is rare that a week goes by without the house being occupied for most of the nights. Usually they come not for the history, but for the ghosts; drawn by the fearsome reputation of the house, many are seeking an encounter with something otherworldly.

Sometimes, they get more than they bargain for.

CHAPTER TWO
"We Want Answers"

In 2010, TV presenters Zak Bagans, Aaron Goodwin, and Nick Groff visited the Moore House in order to shoot an episode of their show *Ghost Adventures*. It's fair to say that *Ghost Adventures* is a show that has a penchant for the dramatic. A case in point: the Villisca episode opens with flashes of an axe slicing through the air, dripping blood everywhere as it chops — the implication being that it is hacking into the body of a helpless victim.

There's a montage of fast cuts: The three stars of the show, standing on the lawn of the Moore House, each of them clutching an axe. The head of an axe, dripping thick, viscous blood from the blade. Front man Bagans emerging from the cellar, again holding an axe, declaring that eight people were hacked to death in their sleep. Whether you're a fan of their methods and style or not, there's no denying that Bagans and company know how to set the stage for a compelling story.

As mentioned previously, there's some debate as to whether the killer broke into the house after the Moore family and their guests were sleeping, or if he was already hiding in the attic when they came home, and was simply biding his time before coming out to strike. Bagans goes with the latter version of the story. After showing the bed in which Mr. and Mrs. Moore were murdered, he leads the camera into the back bedroom upstairs, declaring that four children were killed in there. There's a recreation of sorts, with a faceless male figure seen wandering from room to room, bathed in an eerie red light, swinging away with an axe.

The downstairs bedroom came next. Bagans mentions that the killer "didn't want to see himself," adding that he covered the reflective surfaces inside the house because "he didn't want to see what a monster looked like." As assumptions go, that's not necessarily a bad one in this case.

We are introduced to author and authority on the Villisca murders, Roy Marshall, whose book on the case represents one of the best accounts put into print. He and Bagans are sitting in the Montgomery County Courthouse, where the murder trial took place shortly after the killings.

Bagans names three of the most prominent suspects in the case: Senator Frank Jones, Andy Sawyer, and Reverend George Kelly. In print, Marshall has advocated for Reverend Kelly being the most likely culprit, and Bagans seems happy to go along with that. He seems surprised to hear that the jury didn't believe Kelly's confession. Marshall states his opinion that the investigation into the murders was either "incompetent or corrupt."

"Is that why this house is presumably so damn active with unexplained activity?" Bagans asks, perhaps rhetorically. There's no answer from Roy Marshall, who does not seem to be a believer in the paranormal side of things, based upon comments made in his book to that effect. He also admits to being "very skeptical" of the possibility that new information on the case might be obtained from paranormal sources. I give Mr. Marshall a tip of the hat for that. I respect his insistence on relying purely upon evidence and eyewitness testimony in order to reach his conclusion as to the murderer's identity.

To his credit, Marshall agrees to accompany Bagans, Groff, and Goodwin during a portion of their stay at the house, which suggests that he is willing to keep an open mind on the matter, promising that "if I think it's hogwash, I'll tell you." You can't say fairer than that.

We're introduced to Johnny Houser, who lives next door to the Moore House and has played a significant role its upkeep. Showing a definite talent for understatement, Johnny tells Bagans that "there's something not nice about this place. It definitely has a dark side." He adds that although there is both good and bad energy inside the Villisca Axe Murder House, in his opinion, the good energy is residual — a sort of after-echo, if you will — whereas the bad energy is "intelligent...*highly* intelligent."

As I will come to learn when I meet him in person, Johnny Houser is a cool and down-to-Earth kind of guy. Very matter-of-factly, he tells Zak about the phenomena taking place inside the Moore House suddenly starting to follow him home. As he lives just thirty feet away, in the house next door, it's not as if the energies have very far to travel.

Johnny felt himself turning "mean, cold, bitter toward family members." He attributes this to the influence of the malign forces that occupy the house. When I meet him face to face nine years later, he hasn't changed his mind about that in the slightest.

It's well-known that *Ghost Adventures* loves its demons. They were one of the first TV shows to encounter supposedly demonic cases on an increasingly frequent basis. While I'm not saying that such entities don't exist (remember, there's no such thing as a true expert in the paranormal field) I do believe that non-human entities are a lot less common than is sometimes claimed.

"What percentage of the hauntings here do you think are demonic?" Zak Bagans asks Johnny, leaning against the closet door in the childrens' bedroom upstairs.

Johnny thinks for a second before answering. "If there is demonic in here, it's overpowering everything else at this point."

Always willing to square off against something unpleasant, Bagans challenges the entity to "show us your power," offering to show it respect if it will show them some respect in return. The result is unexpected: the closet door opens up by itself, almost exactly on cue. Is this a case of a spirit responding to Zak's challenge, or simply an old door in an old frame popping open at exactly the right moment? It's impossible to say for sure, but the possibilities are intriguing.

"I have a *really* bad feeling," Johnny says. Zak says that he has one too.

It's worth pointing out that this particular closet door has a history of opening itself. In his book *Murdered in Their Beds: History and Hauntings Of Villisca And The Midwest Ax Murders,* prolific author Troy Taylor recounts his own experience inside the Moore House. He was visiting the house in the company of some ghost hunting enthusiasts, and was hanging back, noting everything that was going on in the way that a good writer tends to do.

Troy witnessed the closet door closing itself on request with his own eyes. This happened not just once, but several times. It was happening when the ghost hunters were trying to coax Paul, one of the murdered Moore children, into interacting with them in exchange for a piece of candy.

Determined to get to the bottom of the mystery, Troy inspected the closet and its door in great detail. He also made sure that there were no open windows that might be causing drafts to enter the house. It made no difference. Once again, the closet door swung shut, and he had no way to account for it.

After a two-hour break, during which time Paul had been

specifically asked not to touch the door, it remained in exactly the same position, ever so slightly ajar. The lady who had been trying to interact with Paul once again offered him candy if he would close the door.

The door opened itself then pushed itself shut again. To this day, Troy Taylor, a man who has spent countless hours researching haunted houses and writing about them, has no satisfactory non-paranormal explanation for what happened with the closet door.

We'll hear more from Troy later.

As the show picks up, Zak Bagans also interviews paranormal investigator Chris Dedman, who suffered what he calls "my night in Hell" inside the house. He tells an apparently fascinated Bagans about the time he used a Spirit Box in the parlor, attempting to contact some of the entities that were said to haunt the house by asking them who was present. A voice came through the speaker which may have been saying the name "Reverend Kelly."

Commanding the voice to tell him who it was, Chris received a response which he believes said the word "Legion." This, of course, is the name of a demonic entity referred to in the Bible, more specifically in the book of Mark, when Jesus was said to cast out this dark spirit from a man that it was possessing.

Then Jesus asked him, "what is your name?" "My name is Legion," he replied, "for we are many."

As any experienced paranormal investigator will tell you, EVPs and direct voice phenomena are highly subjective things. You can give ten different investigators a copy of the same EVP, and they will most likely come up with ten different (often *very* different) interpretations of the same piece of audio recording. The *Ghost Adventures* episode plays both of these snippets, and I invite you to watch it and judge for yourself what you think they say. My personal opinion is that the "Reverend Kelly" soundbite does indeed sound like the word "Kelly" (I don't hear "Reverend" at all) but that "Legion" is a little harder to make out. It sounds more like "legend" to my ear.

Chris describes getting to his feet, walking out of the house, and standing outside, having just gotten the wind knocked out of him by some kind of force that he could not see. What Chris and his fellow investigator describe happening to him is nothing less than a full-fledged physical attack. A subsequent examination showed a series of three long, irregular scratches running down the length of his back.

Some people believe that the number three is significant when it comes to scratch marks, because it is said to mock the Holy Trinity of Father, Son, and Holy Ghost. It's an interesting theory, and while it doesn't fit with my own personal belief system, that doesn't mean that it has no merit.

Zak's next interviewee is Linda, a former resident of the house, a lady who lived there with her parents and siblings as a child. He also brings in her sister, Patty. With the exception of Johnny Houser, paranormal investigators come and go, spending a night here and a night there inside the house, but always ultimately packing up and moving on after a relatively short period of time. The eyewitness testimony of somebody who actually *lived* inside the Moore House for longer than a brief spell is therefore worth its weight in gold.

The two sisters heard the sound of a little girl's voice in the front room of the house (the parlor), where they slept at night. This would have been immediately adjacent to the small bedroom in which the two Stillinger girls had been murdered. Their mother put it down to nothing more than her daughters having an active imagination, but they were certain about what they had heard.

Of far more concern was something which happened to their father when he was honing a knife in the kitchen one day. For safety purposes, it's important to sharpen a blade away from one's body, rather than toward it. That's exactly what he was doing when some kind of invisible force seemed to take hold of his arm, redirect it, and cause it to stab the startled man in the chest.

It's a deeply troubling incident, and it might be tempting for some people to write the whole thing off as being nothing more than a tall tale, if it weren't for the fact that it would happen *again* decades later, in 2014.

Assuming that this was caused by some kind of negative entity, what would be the motivation? According to Linda, it's because this dark spirit "doesn't want anybody here. This is *his* house."

To whom is she referring? None other than the murderer himself.

Linda believes that the spirit of the killer is haunting the house. It's a claim that, frankly, makes little sense to me. For one thing, the murderer did not die inside the house. Two adults and six children did, all of them at his hands, but this man — whoever he was — walked away Scot free and never looked back. So why, then, would he haunt the Villisca Axe Murder House if he did not die there? It's a question that we will return to later in this book.

There are numerous instances on record of people experiencing strange physical symptoms inside the house. Unexplained nausea, headaches, and generalized weakness are three of the more common problems that visitors have reported. Part way through her interview, Linda is forced to sit down on the staircase because she suddenly feels very weak. Zak squats down and takes the time to make sure that she's okay. She is obviously being affected emotionally, something which many others have also felt when entering the property.

A tearful Linda explains that the house "has been with me my whole life, it calls me back..." This is something that I have seen at a number of haunted locations. Indeed, I have also experienced this effect myself. Some people seem to develop a great affinity for certain places, returning to them again and again, searching for answers to the mysteries which surround them. A strong connection is formed between place and person, one which manifests as a compulsion to keep on going back.

Zak brings out a voice recorder and asks thin air if it will speak to him "in order to help give Linda closure." He is rewarded with a Class B EVP, what sounds like a staccato male voice saying the words, *Where is she?*

It's an intriguing find. When the two sisters finally leave the house, they are clearly quite upset.

Now it's time for their lockdown to begin. Static cameras are set up in multiple different locations. One is positioned in the cellar; the second is located in the ground floor bedroom in which the Stillinger girls were killed. Camera three goes in the attic. Number four is set to cover the children's bedroom upstairs.

When night falls, Roy Marshall joins the group inside the house. As there is no electric lighting inside the property, this portion of the show is shot in night vision. Zak begins with an EVP session in the Stillingers' bedroom. It bears no fruit, so they move upstairs to the master bedroom. More sessions are conducted in different parts of the house.

With Roy keeping a watchful eye on things, the crew relocates to the barn in order to review the audio evidence. The microphone seems to have captured a gruff male voice. Although it's difficult to make out with any real clarity, they believe that the invisible speaker is saying the words *I killed six kids*.

What's most fascinating about this is its accuracy. Six children were indeed killed inside the house: the four Moore Children, and the two visiting Stillinger girls. Six is, of course, a very specific number in relation to the Villisca Axe Murder House, and I don't believe that this finding is any sort of coincidence.

But it's not nearly as impressive as what happens inside the empty house while everybody is over at the barn. One of the remote cameras is activated, and it records the sound of three distinct footsteps walking on the hardwood floor. Fascinating, but nothing compared to the attic door slamming violently shut. The door is wide open and flush with the wall. It swings 180 degrees to close itself, a split second after the last footstep is heard.

A skeptic might be tempted to dismiss this as a freak draft. I couldn't disagree more. I would go on to spend four days and nights inside that house. There is practically nothing in the way of airflow. The second floor can be almost unbearably hot in the summer because of this. Even a strong wind outside the house would not be able to slam the attic door as aggressively as this. It's a truly impressive evidence capture. I've no reason whatsoever to believe that it might be faked, particularly as an objective third party — Roy Marshall — was in the house along with the *Ghost Adventures* team for much of the evening. For me, this is the standout piece of evidence from the episode, and it gives me genuine goosebumps to think that before long, I'll be taking up residence in that exact same house.

Johnny Houser locks the team back inside the house. This time, they lead off with a Spirit Box session in the front room. The Spirit Box hops from one radio frequency to another at a very fast sweep rate. Some people believe that disembodied entities can communicate with us by "jumping in" and speaking in the gaps between those frequencies. It's a controversial device, one which has as many detractors as it does supporters, but sometimes it can yield intriguing results.

One of the big downsides is that the words coming through such boxes are often unclear and difficult to make out. The first intelligible word we're shown in this episode sounds like *Lena.* Lena Stillinger was, of course, one of the two children killed in the back bedroom, just a few feet away from where the *Ghost Adventures* team are conducting their session. It's a solid catch.

Shortly afterward, they get what sounds like another child's voice. They claim that the voice is saying *Wanna play?* I agree with them that the voice seems to be that of a young child, but disagree with their interpretation — I think that the sounds are too indistinct to be clearly labeled.

Zak asks whether this is a little kid that lives at the house, and if so, what is its name? *Paul,* we are told by the on-screen caption. Again, a potentially strong hit. It does indeed sound like *Paul,* which is all the more impressive when one considers that poor Paul Moore, just five years old, was murdered in the upstairs bedroom.

Going for broke, Bagans goes on to ask the name of the killer. What comes back is garbled almost beyond incomprehension. He believes that it says *Andy,* which fits with one of the murder suspects, Andy Sawyer. Unfortunately, despite agreeing with Zak's take on the *Lena* and *Paul* EVPs, I'm not buying this one. That's purely my opinion, of course, and I encourage you to watch the episode and form your own opinion after listening to the EVPs for yourself.

Aaron Goodwin spends the next segment of the show locked in the cellar alone. I give him a lot of credit for letting himself be put in this situation. It's a vulnerable place to be, alone in the dark, locked inside the cellar of one of Iowa's (if not the country's) most haunted houses. If things go bad, it will take Johnny Houser time to come to the rescue and pop the lock to the cellar door.

Zak, for his part, is kneeling in the attic, with Nick filming him. Zak's holding what some claim to be the actual murder weapon, an axe borrowed from the house's owner, Darwin Linn.

"Is this the axe that you used to kill eight people...?" he asks, holding up the axe with one hand. The voice recorder being held in his other hand picks up what Zak states is an EVP, "the sound of an evil spirit laughing." To be completely honest, in my opinion, it's just as likely to be static as it is to be an intelligent response to his question.

Taking things to the next level, Zak lays on his back on the attic floor and props the axe up so that it is standing vertically, its gleaming blade directly in line with his face. No matter how you look at it, this is a gutsy thing to do. There is solid video evidence to suggest that something inside the Villisca Axe Murder House is capable of exerting enough physical force to slam the attic door — so toppling a precariously-balanced axe so that it falls into the face of a

TV presenter ought to be child's play by comparison. (One can't help but think that the Travel Channel's Risk Assessment manager must have had palpitations when they finally saw this footage!)

Nick has his back to the wall in the hallway outside. In addition to filming Zak, he also has a voice recorder running throughout the session. It picks up what sounds like a sinister voice speaking in response to Zak. I agree with about half of the *Ghost Adventures* interpretation of what's said: *We're gonna keep them in the dark.* I definitely hear *we're gonna keep them,* but I'm not sure about the rest. Either way, it's another impressive catch. The Villisca Axe Murder House is by no means a disappointment for them so far.

Zak asks whether he's talking to the real killer, and wants to know why he killed the children. The resulting EVP is a Class B- or a C, in my estimation. According to the show, it says, *'cause they don't step in heaven yet.* I'm not so sure about that, but it's undeniably a voice that is saying *something,* and it does have the weirdness of cadence that is characteristic of so many genuine EVPs.

Nick's recorder also captures an EVP that is spoken in a more childlike voice. *Herman's gonna get you,* is the show's interpretation. I definitely concur that the first word is *Herman*, but find the remainder of the sentence hard to decipher. Still, the house has been a treasure trove of EVPs for the *Ghost Adventures* team. Whether you agree with their assessment of what has actually been said or not is almost irrelevant, and rather misses the point. What matters, first and foremost, is that these anomalous voice messages even exist at all, and I'm hoping that we'll experience similar results when we first visit the Villisca Axe Murder House in person.

CHAPTER THREE
"Be Very Careful in this House."

Another TV show that gave its own take on the Villisca Axe Murder House is *The Dead Files*, in which psychic medium Amy Allan and retired NYPD homicide detective Steve DiSchiavi team up to investigate haunted locations. The premise of the show is that DiSchiavi goes in first to interview witnesses and conduct research, in the manner of a cop investigating a crime; Allan then goes in cold, using her special abilities in order to gather sensory impressions concerning the haunting.

DiSchiavi and Allan make for a good contrast to one another. When combined, their two very different styles always make for interesting and entertaining television.

When it comes to the matter of integrity, I've yet to see any credible accusations of fraud and fakery against this particular show. With no disrespect at all intended to Ms. Allan, who has a solid reputation from what I've heard, the presence of a professionally-trained homicide investigator is a very welcome factor that lends *The Dead Files* a little extra credibility in my eyes. One hopes that if there was any actual fraud associated with the show, a former detective would be quick to put a stop to it, or at the very least speak up publicly.

To their credit, neither of them pretends to be completely

in the dark about the particulars of the case. There's a wealth of information about the Villisca Axe Murders out there on the Internet. DiSchiavi points out that nobody has ever been brought to justice for the killings, and it seems as if this could perhaps be a great opportunity for somebody like Amy Allan to shed some new light on this very cold case.

The crux of the episode is that Johnny Houser is experiencing paranormal activity at his own home, and is hoping that Steve and Amy can help him get to the bottom of it all. Amy is kept in the dark about the fact that she'll be asked to do a walk-through of Johnny's home too, in addition to providing her assessment of the Villisca Axe Murder House.

Steve's first stop is the Moore House, where he meets with Johnny and gets a little background information. Johnny freely admits that the murders have become something of a personal obsession with him, which is quite understandable considering the amount of time he has spent inside the house, and the countless hours he has devoted to researching the crimes which took place there. How can one *not* get a little obsessed under circumstances like that?

Despite the show having been shot in 2013, the interior of the Villisca Axe Murder House looks almost identical to the way it does on my first visit five years later. Johnny gives Steve the grand tour, starting with the Stillinger bedroom downstairs. He describes a number of physical symptoms being experienced in there, such as pain in the neck and back, nausea, and generalized sickness going on. Now, members of his own family are suffering from these exact same conditions in their home next door.

"I'm concerned that something over here followed me next door," he reveals. "I have a wife, a 13-year-old, a 4-year-old, and we're getting scared of some of the things that are happening..."

Some of the physical phenomena occurring at Johnny's place mirror those which also happen inside the Moore house, such as the doors opening and closing themselves. This happens in many hauntings, and isn't necessarily something to be concerned about, but far more ominous are the growls and scratching sounds that's he's heard coming from the Stillinger bedroom — sounds that have now started to follow Johnny back to his home. It's almost as if he caught some kind of paranormal contagion at the Axe Murder House, and took it back with him to unwittingly infect the rest of his family.

What interests me about the growls is the way Johnny describes them as sounding neither human nor animal, and being followed by a female either gasping or moaning.

To his credit, Steve DiSchiavi doesn't shy away from asking the difficult questions. Being polite but forthright, he asks Johnny if his knowledge of two young girls having been murdered in the same room could perhaps have biased him.

It's a fair comment. Johnny is absolutely convinced that what he heard was one hundred percent real, and sticks to his guns, as he still does to this day.

The next stop is over at Johnny's house. The home was once the residence of Mary Peckham, the neighbor who first realized that something seemed "off" about the Moore House early on the morning of June 10, 1912. Mary died six months after the axe murders, with a nervous breakdown thought to have been a contributory factor.

Johnny tells Steve that he was all alone in the house one morning, and very clearly heard a voice call out "John!" After calling out to Mary Peckham and asking for her (or anything else associated with the Axe Murder House) to open a door, the door immediately flew open on command.

DiSchiavi's narration tells us that he finds Johnny's story a little far-fetched, but isn't seeing any clear signs that he isn't telling the truth. It won't be long before Steve's partner, Amy Allan, will arrive to lend some credence to Johnny's claims.

Steve's next interviewee is Kristy, who also gives tours of the Villisca Axe Murder House. Throughout the show, Johnny has seemed perfectly relaxed, even when recounting some extremely frightening experiences. Kristy is very much the opposite, something which the former detective immediately picks up on.

"I don't like being upstairs," Kristy admits, clearly more

than a little unnerved by her surroundings. The upper floor has been the more active of the two, in her experience. While giving a tour of the house to several members of the public, she distinctly heard the sound of footsteps coming up the wooden staircase, despite the fact that every one of her charges was already up on the second floor. One of the customers on the tour came forward and said that he just had heard the same footsteps himself.

Kristy also claims to have been affected physically, touched on several parts of her body, some of which were extremely inappropriate. It's easy to see why she feels less than comfortable inside the house, and she is quick to accept Steve's offer to get out of the building.

It's hard to blame her for that.

When Amy arrives at the location, she immediately claims to make contact with an angry, disfigured woman — angry, Amy claims, because she allowed somebody in that she shouldn't have. Presumably, this could be Sara Moore, whose face was severely disfigured during the axe attack. Then she "hears from someone else that it's actually her husband's fault."

Assuming that the "it" in question is the murder spree itself, then this could mean that the feud which grew up between Josiah Moore and Frank Jones lay at the heart of why all eight occupants of the house were killed. Although I find it doubtful that Jones hired somebody to kill the entire Moore family, there are those who believe that this is exactly what took place.

Inside the Stillinger bedroom, Amy picks up on "two females, maybe eight or nine." Despite the fact that the production team has removed pictures of the Moores and Stillingers from the house in advance of her visit, it's a very well-known fact that the two girls were murdered in the only downstairs bedroom. It's a piece of information that could have been found on the Internet in less than a minute. This is where it gets a little more interesting. Amy adds that one of the two girls like to scare people by growling at them. Not only would this information help explain the growls that Johnny Houser has heard in that same room, but it will also come into play during my own investigation of the house in a manner that I can't yet foresee.

Amy mimics a little girl growling, showing her teeth and making claws out of her fingers. "I feel like they would hear her and feel her before they saw her." Again, this is consistent with Johnny's experience. To my knowledge, he has not seen any apparitions inside the Villisca Axe Murder House. Yet another hit comes immediately afterward, as Amy describes there being a lot of pain in her left flank and lower-back — the very same back pain that Johnny has experienced himself while inside the house, and which usually goes away the minute he steps foot outside.

Johnny's friends must be less than comfortable with staying over at his place after the frightening experience one of them had, waking up to see the disfigured face of an old woman floating just inches away from his own, staring right back at him. Understandably, the man flatly refused to spend another night staying there.

We all know that children have imaginary friends. Many of us who investigate claims of ghosts and hauntings have come to the conclusion that not all of them are actually imaginary. This probably goes for the lady named Hattie that Johnny's three-year-old daughter has described seeing upstairs in her home.

Little is made of Hattie in the episode. Only later would new information come to light about her. Although it isn't mentioned in the show, the little girl soon reached the point at which she refused to go upstairs to bed because Hattie was "being mean" to her.

A little historical research turned up something both ominous and fascinating. Following the death of Mary Peckham shortly after the murders took place, the house was willed to her adult daughter...

...one Hattie Peckham. This was something that neither Johnny nor his family had been aware of when the mysterious Hattie first starting making an appearance.

Finally, Johnny's daughter stopped mentioning Hattie. Her father breathed a big sigh of relief, simply assuming that was the end of that. He was giving his two-year-old son a bath one day, and the toddler was listing all of the names of the people he knew, then saying goodbye to them.

"Bye, Mom. Bye, Dad. Bye, Sace. Bye, Hattie."

Johnnie's eyes went wide. Where had he gotten *that* name from?

A few years later, Johnny's daughter asked him if he still remembered Hattie. He nodded warily, half-anticipating that something terrible was about to come out of her mouth.

"That was weird," she said. Johnny smiled.

"What do you remember?" he asked her.

"She'd stare at me while I was sleeping."

That brought him some small measure of comfort. After giving the matter some thought, he ultimately concluded that if Hattie Peckham was standing over his daughter's bed and watching her while she slept, she was probably a protective spirit, keeping a maternal eye on the current generation of children growing up in what had once been her home. What the child had perceived to be meanness on Hattie's part could simply have been the stern affect that many people had back in those days, particularly around the children of others.

On her walkthrough of Johnny's house, Amy declares that many of the dead people from next door (i.e. the Moore House) come over, and that some even reside there. This is said to be because they are happier at Johnny's place, and like to come together there. That makes sense to me. The energies over at the Villisca Axe Murder House have to be significantly less pleasant than they would be in an active family dwelling, or so one would hope. It's hard to imagine spirits wanting to hang out and enjoy some fellowship in a house which has been tainted by such an evil act.

Things take a turn for the weird when the woman encountered by Amy outside begins raging at another spirit from Johnny's place, "going crazy," in Amy's words. She goes on to say that the woman "has had it with the living" and that all of her anger is directed at one individual, an adult male, and this is making her scream at him that "You're a guilty motherfucker and you know it!"

That's a very visceral response to have, and one would assume that it's directed toward the killer himself.

Amy says that the woman's apparition has been seen over at the Houser residence many times, which suggests that it could be Hattie, the female apparition who has been seen repeatedly by Johnny's daughter. With Amy describing the specter as "not looking normal, she's all messed up," it seems likely that this is the same apparition as the one which scared Johnny's overnight guest into never returning again

— but there's a problem here. Hattie Peckham's face was never "all messed up." On the other hand, Sara Moore's *was*.

As the show progresses, Amy begins to make the case that what's actually being haunted isn't so much the Villisca Axe Murder House itself, but rather, the Houser family. It's an intriguing possibility, and I must confess, one that I had never really considered until now.

Delving further into the motivations of the angry woman, Amy says that she wants those who are still alive to suffer some measure of the same pain which she herself constantly experiences.

Standing outside the Moore House, Amy reports seeing a man standing there, watching the house — somebody "very religious." It's likely that she is already aware of the fact that Reverend Kelly is considered a prime suspect in the case, but that doesn't necessarily mean that she isn't sensing exactly what she claims to be sensing. The information is out there in the public domain, however, so most skeptics would dismiss this as probably not being paranormally-obtained knowledge.

She ultimately picks up on there having been some kind of conspiracy behind the murders, with four male co-conspirators involved. Presenting her findings to Johnny and to Kristy, Amy tells them that she can't believe so many of the spirits are still there. She picks up on some of the specific body pains and aches that Johnny has been experiencing, which makes for a fairly impressive hit.

Amy then goes on to describe the "short, pale, very spiteful" female spirit that was full of rage. The woman, Amy claims, was a murder victim, and felt responsible for the crime taking place, but also blamed her husband for it. The only woman this could possibly have been was, of course, Sara Moore. When Steve shows Amy a picture of Mrs. Moore, the medium positively identifies her as being the same woman. Again, it must be pointed out that photographs of the entire Moore family are freely available on the Internet, not least on the website of the Villisca Axe Murder House itself. I'm not saying that Amy cheated; I'm saying that this information is something that was readily accessible, and so it could quite easily have a mundane explanation.

Steve brings up the point that Sara Moore was singled out to receive her death blows from the axe blade, rather than the flat head. Could this go some way toward explaining why her spirit might be so angry?

Changing tack, we next hear about two girls Amy claims to have picked up on in the downstairs bedroom. This would, of course, be Lena and Ina Stillinger. "One girl specifically enjoys interacting with the living," she says. In what looks like another solid hit, Amy adds that the little girl likes to growl at people — something that Johnny has experienced himself in that very same room.

Steve shows her pictures of Ina and Lena Stillinger. Amy believes that Lena is the girl responsible for the growling, which she does out of a desire to get some attention — a perfectly understandable way for an 11-year-old girl to behave.

Ultimately, as with many other mediums who have visited the house, Amy isn't able to provide any clear insight into what exactly happened on the night of the murders. She claims to have heard a man say that everything was going to be okay, followed by a different voice saying "There's no place to run."

Amy reports seeing Lena being dragged across the room by her leg. Recall that Lena's body was found with a bloody smear on her leg, something which the bodies of the other victims lacked. Amy picks up on some confusion coming from Lena, who she thinks knew her killer. A man's voice says, "Make sure they're all dead."

Next, Amy sees Sara Moore standing in a corner of the upstairs bedroom, clutching one of her children and screaming "Why aren't you doing anything? How can you let them do this?" This is followed by the killer responding that this wasn't how it was all supposed to happen, implying that the entire family was not supposed to be murdered. In other words, the killing was a botched job.

Full credit to Steve for disagreeing with Amy here. Considering his background as a homicide cop, he's well-suited to offer up an informed opinion on something like this. After outlining four of the best-known suspects, Steve emphasizes the weight of evidence against Reverend George Kelly, including the confession made during his interrogation.

Amy says that Kelly was the spirit she met in the barn, a short, thin, pale-looking man (that classic English complexion). She adds that he really enjoyed "torturing them," though this is never expanded upon, and none of the victims' bodies showed any signs of having been tortured. She then presents a sketch that she did of this man, who does indeed look eerily like the photograph of Reverend Kelly when they are placed side-by-side for comparison.

She's quick to emphasize that, although she's convinced the man she encountered really was Kelly, he wasn't the only one involved with the killing. Kristy agrees, voicing something that has often been pointed out by critics of the various "one killer" theories: how can just one man have killed everybody in the house, without any help?

Steve's view is that, in his experience, serial killers rarely act with accomplices. He's absolutely correct about that. Although there are some instances of killers working in partnership, or having a weak-willed individual assist them, these are the relatively rare exceptions. However, he's impressed enough with Amy's past track record as a medium that he's willing to go along with her conspiracy theory this time, as he can't find any evidence that either proves or disproves it.

Let's give Amy the benefit of the doubt for a minute and take a closer look at what this might mean in the context of the Villisca Axe Murders. Firstly, Amy's claim that Lena Stillinger knew her killer. It's unlikely that she knew any of the other major suspects, but she could easily have seen George Kelly at the church service earlier that evening. His face may well have been fresh in her mind.

What of the claim that Sara Moore was screaming "Why aren't you doing anything?" She's unlikely to have yelled this at George Kelly, and far more likely to have done so if Frank Jones had been present in the house. Sara would have been familiar with Jones as her husband's former employer. As to who the other co-conspirators might have been, we are given no real insight. Albert, Jones' son, would be a logical candidate, if the rumors that had circulated around the townsfolk about Josiah Moore having inappropriate contact with his wife are to be believed. Might they also have brought along some hired muscle? If so, who could be trusted to keep quiet in the face of such a brutal murder, involving not just a man, but also a woman and six children? It would have to have been a callous individual indeed.

Next, Amy turns her attention to Johnny's home. She tells him that most of the family hang out downstairs in his house, just because it's so nice in there. "If I were you, I'd be very careful in this house," she warns Johnny. "It's pretty intense." Sara Moore is extremely angry, she adds, claiming that the spirit of the murdered woman is full of rage and ready to lash out at the living who, in her mind, "deserve it."

Johnny's impression is a little different. He finds the lower floor of his home to be tranquil, but the second floor is less so, being prone to doors opening and slamming shut all by themselves, and the sound of phantom footsteps. One is forced to wonder whether the woman seen by his daughter in the upstairs bedroom is the spirit of Sara Moore. Certainly, the apparition that scared away his friend fits the description very well.

The show ends with a fairly damning verdict. Amy states that the Villisca Axe Murder House needs to stop being a tourist attraction, because if it does not, the spirits of the murder victims will never truly be laid to rest. This may be a valid point to make. For his part, Johnny counters that his intentions and those of Martha, the owner, are not in the least bit disrespectful of what the Moore family and Stillinger sisters suffered inside the house. The tours given by Johnny and Christy are helping to keep their memory alive, after all, ensuring that they are never forgotten. One can perhaps question whether this is a double-edged sword, and if it might be keeping the victims somehow tied to the house and locality.

Yet we do go out on a positive note. Amy tells Johnny

that he was specifically chosen to play a role at the Villisca Axe Murder House, implying that he was drawn there in order to serve some greater purpose. She concludes by claiming that telling the story of the house's history to visitors will help bring the murder victims peace..."at least, for now." We are told that, since modifying the content of his tours to minimize references to the paranormal, the activity at Johnny's house has now stopped.

As the show was shot five years before my upcoming visit to Villisca, I'm curious as to whether this is still the case. I guess I'll just have to ask the man himself.

CHAPTER FOUR
"I Didn't do it to Myself."

In early November of 2014, multiple news outlets began to report a very disturbing story. The headlines all ran with some variation of *Ghost Hunter Stabs Self Inside "Haunted" Axe Murder House.*

The facts of the case are that on Friday, November 7, a 37-year-old male was treated by first responders at the Villisca Axe Murder House for a single stab wound to the chest — a stab wound that, by the man's own admission, was self-inflicted. The incident took place in the downstairs bedroom at approximately half past midnight, which some people leapt at the opportunity to point out was the approximate time of the Villisca Axe Murders.

The police officers that responded to the scene quickly ruled out the idea of there having been an assailant, an outsider who had gained entry to the house somehow and had attacked the man. The house had been rented for the night by the man's parents. He was completely alone in the house at the time of the stabbing, and would later state that he had done his best to recreate the crime scene inside the property, presumably in an attempt to stimulate paranormal activity into taking place. The consequences could easily have turned out to be tragic, but fortunately he survived his injuries after being flown by helicopter to a regional trauma center in Omaha, Nebraska, and receiving expert medical care.

Like many visitors to the Villisca Axe Murder House, the gentleman in question had driven from out of state — in this case, coming in from Wisconsin. At the time the incident first made the news, I reacted in the same way as the rest of the paranormal community: there was a degree of shock at what had happened, and great relief that the man had survived his potentially-fatal injury. But I was also curious as to *why* this terrifying situation had arisen in the first place.

There are some eerie parallels here with *The Ghost Adventures* episode in which the two ladies who had lived in the house when they were growing up had watched as their father, sharpening a knife in the kitchen, suddenly had some kind of unseen force take control of his hand, forcing him to stab himself with the blade.

The two stabbing incidents, although separated by decades, both took place within just a few feet of one another inside the Moore House. Just how likely is it that this was a coincidence? It's certainly possible, I suppose, but the more years that I spend in the field of paranormal research, the less of a believer in coincidence I have become.

Although a number of people report having been scratched and suffering inexplicable, usually superficial injuries at the Villisca Axe Murder House, this is the only potentially life-threatening incident that I am aware of. Once it had dropped out of the news headlines, I fully expected the incident to disappear into obscurity, becoming another curious footnote in the history of a very strange building.

That changed in 2019 when the TV show *Kindred Spirits* aired an episode that was filmed on location in Villisca. In the episode, TV stars Amy Bruni, Adam Berry, and Chip Coffey not only spent time inside the Moore House, but they also interviewed the gentleman who had stabbed himself.

Before that, we're introduced to another paranormal investigator named John, and told that he now believes himself to be cursed after what happened to him inside the Villisca Axe Murder House one night. This man refuses to set foot inside the house again, choosing to meet with Amy and Adam inside the barn instead.

John's story is indeed a disturbing one. He visited the house along with several friends. An audio recording session took a turn for the sinister when an EVP told them to *leave at once.* It was followed by another which said *just kill John,* and added his surname.

John and a number of his friends and family members experienced some very unfortunate occurrences over the next few months, including a number of unanticipated medical emergencies and even deaths. It's hard to watch this interview without one's heart going out to John, and feeling sympathy for the losses he suffered after spending the night at the Villisca Axe Murder House. His stated purpose in returning to meet Amy and Adam is to make sure that he was not in some way responsible for those tragedies because of his prior visit to the house.

Belief is a very powerful thing, and John clearly believes that there might be a link between his time at Villisca and what happened to his loved ones. It is not for me to say whether that is or is not the case. However, one certainly cannot doubt the depth and sincerity of his conviction.

Adam tells us that they have to find out if the Villisca axe murderer was responsible for this, adding that the spirit could have somehow attached itself to John. I find this to be a curious leap for them to make. To assume that the killer himself is the culprit, when we know that he did not die in the house and most likely never even returned there after committing the murders, seems a little premature to me. I'm not saying that they're wrong, necessarily, but I do think it's important to keep an open mind about such things, particularly if you're conducting a paranormal investigation.

After setting up surveillance equipment, the duo proceeds to carry out an EVP session in the parlor. In order to try and make contact, Amy plays the EVP obtained by John, the one that he believes says, *just kill John (surname)*. To be completely honest, and with no disrespect intended, that's not at all what I hear. In fact, I do not hear any intelligible words at all.

Amy asks if there is something bad in the house that they should be worried about. Almost immediately, a hard-to-make-out noise, something akin to quiet murmuring, is heard from elsewhere in the house. Adam believes that it could have been the voice of a man. This is not without precedent at Villisca. In fact, a number of visitors have reported experiencing something very similar.

Moving up to the second floor yields no results, so Amy and Adam take a break and leave the house in order to meet Buck, the man who was found with the knife sticking out of his chest back in 2014. I give Buck a great deal of credit for his willingness to recount what must have been a deeply traumatizing experience.

Buck's parents had indeed hired the house for the evening as a birthday gift, just as the newspaper reports said. It is also true that Buck did his best to recreate the crime scene, although he did not incorporate an axe into it – rather fortunately, as things turned out. When his attempts to contact the spirits of the Villisca Axe Murder House went unheeded, Buck's manner became increasingly provocative (in his own words, he was being "very vulgar."). As some paranormal investigators have learned to their cost, this can be a dangerous gambit — one that can sometimes come back to bite you.

After looking up at what he describes as "the biggest orb

I've ever seen," Buck suddenly became aware of the knife now impaled in his shoulder. It had penetrated all the way through to his lung. He remembers nothing between that moment and waking up in hospital, restrained to a bed and intubated with a breathing tube.

"I do remember this," Buck insists, "*I didn't do it to myself.* There is *something* there..." He says that his stepfather and mother recorded an EVP that whispered, *Don't worry about Buck. We'll get him.* However, he adds that they wiped the EVP and no copy of it survives.

Amy plays him the *just kill John* EVP, and Buck finds it deeply unnerving. Surprisingly, he is still willing to accompany Amy and Adam back to the Villisca Axe Murder House. He leads them into the Stillinger bedroom, and lays back on the bed where the stabbing took place. It's chilling to watch Buck relive the harrowing incident in the exact same spot where it happened.

Afterward, Johnny Houser drops by to share some of his own experiences with the house. He gives Amy and Adam a few suggestions on how best to investigate, and then they leave Adam in the house alone. Amy monitors him from the barn. He sits outside the Moore childrens' bedroom, close to the attic entrance, and begins asking questions. Something taps the recorder, he claims.

"Did you do something to the family?" Adam asks. Amy insists that a voice replies "I killed them." Against, I must respectfully disagree. Although *something* does indeed turn up on the audio, in my opinion it's far from intelligible.

They both hear what Adam describes as "major, *major*" movement somewhere in the house. "We now have our own evidence that the axe murderer is here," Amy declares, "and that he continues to prey on vulnerable visitors." I think that this is leaping to a conclusion that the evidence does not necessarily support.

She heads upstairs, hearing a noise from the empty attic just before she steps inside. "I think you're a terrible person," Amy begins, taking a seat in the center of the floor. "I hope you're burning and rotting in Hell…"

Amy continues in this vein, prodding and goading whatever haunts the house. When she checks her voice recorder at the end of the session, a gruff male voice can be heard, saying what the show claims is *"Fuck you!"* It's difficult to judge for oneself, because the profanity has been bleeped out. The most that we, the viewer, can make out is what might be the word "you"…or might not.

Psychic medium Chip Coffey is the final visitor of the week. He picks up on the presence of "a monster" and identifies the room "where the two little girls were killed" correctly. While Mr. Coffey may possibly be obtaining this information via psychic impressions, it's also true that this information is freely available in the public domain, and a small memorial plaque in that room bears the names of Lena and Ina Stillinger, plus their ages. We do not know for sure whether that information was removed prior to his arrival, or whether it was even removed at all. The reader should note that I am by no means accusing Mr. Coffey of anything improper, merely trying to cover as many of the various different possibilities as I can — something one is always wise to do when extraordinary claims are involved.

Chip states that he does not feel those who were killed, but that he does pick up on "him that did it," and "this sick, psychosexual perverse sense of doing it. He got off on this." On this, I most definitely agree. That's a very reasonable conclusion to derive from a murder in which an entire family were bludgeoned to death for no apparent reason, a pre-teen girl was sexually objectified and potentially molested, and a piece of meat was probably used for an abhorrent sexual purpose.

"He was so unbelievably calm," the medium continues, standing in the attic doorway. Chip picks up on the killer's willingness to wait as long as it takes, presumably for the Moore family and their guests to come back from church and fall asleep, and his sheer, giddy excitement at the prospect of killing them all.

At the conclusion of the episode, Chip escorts John, who was so troubled by his experiences at Villisca, back inside the house. The idea, we're told, is to help him confront his fears and hopefully emerge all the stronger for it. Chip conducts a personal reading for John in the barn, and appears to bring him some comfort.

As the credits roll, I'm still not sure I agree with the assertion that the killer is necessarily responsible for the haunting. It's important to keep an open mind, and consider a number of alternative possibilities before coming to a conclusion. More evidence is needed before I can form an educated opinion, and going in search of that evidence has just become my primary focus.

It's time to experience the Villisca Axe Murder House for myself.

CHAPTER FIVE
Uninvited Guests

It's not understating things to say that 2020 has been a dumpster fire of a year. Around Christmastime, the first reports regarding a new type of virus started turning up in the media. Despite warnings that it could potentially be very serious, most people in the United States just blew it off. Most of the initial cases were coming from China, which seemed so far away that it was completely removed from everyday life.

Things picked up steam quickly. By the time winter gave way to spring, the novel coronavirus named Covid-19 was all anybody wanted to talk about. The disease soon spread, hitting cities like New York brutally hard. As the death toll began to mount, states began to lock themselves down. There were curfews, emergency health orders, and social distancing. Some were told to quarantine.

It's now the summer of 2020. As a paramedic, I've spent the first half of the year working on the front lines and also behind them, splitting my time between the ambulance operations center and getting in as much street time as I can.

I've been in the emergency medical profession for eighteen years, but I'm still having trouble adjusting to the so-called 'new normal.' It's the little things that I miss. We don't shake hands anymore; instead, EMS crews bump elbows when we say hi to one another. We wear masks all the time, whether out in public or sitting in the cab of our ambulance.

Looming over everything, there's the ever-present fear of contracting Covid-19. There's no such thing as a routine 911 call anymore. Every patient gets a surgical mask, in order to try and contain any potential contamination. We wear medical-grade N95 face masks on every call, along with gloves, eye protection, and often, gowns and face shields. Practicing medicine has become hot, sweaty, and frustrating work, taking twice the time that it used to.

Millions of people are out of a job. Many are losing their homes. Vacations and business trips are pretty much canceled. Traveling outside the U.S. is next to impossible, and few people are flying from state to state. Economically speaking, the airline industry is in freefall, and the entire hotel/hospitality injury isn't far behind.

For the first time I can remember, I've done just one paranormal investigation and research trip in the first half of the year: the haunted Bellaire House in Ohio. That was six months ago, and by now I'm just itching to get back out into the field. Big, heavily trafficked locations are out of the question, as is spending time around sizable groups of people.

But then, there's Villisca.

After giving the matter some thought, I realize that it

should be easy to socially distance inside the Moore House. It's small and self-contained. If I keep my team to the barest of minimums, then make sure that we all wear masks and are scrupulous with our handwashing, then I'm convinced that I can lower the risk of infection to acceptable levels.

Bearing that in mind, I take just one colleague along with me — my friend and partner in crime, Sarah. I'm convinced that the pair of us can operate safely as a group for the two nights in which we have full access to the house.

Just like that, it's happening. I start out on the long drive in the early hours of a Wednesday morning. There's something peaceful, almost soothing about traveling across the empty plains of eastern Colorado and rural Nebraska underneath a starry night sky.

Lightning batters the horizon off to the south, giving me a spectacular light show through the passenger-side window. There's little traffic on the roads at this hour of the morning, and with the cruise control engaged, I'm starting to think about what the coming 48 hours might have in store for us.

You only have to look at the news to see that large segments of society have been coming unglued. People are becoming angrier and more cynical than they have been in a long time. Irritation, intolerance, and rudeness are at record highs in the America of 2020. Pretty much any negative emotion you care to name is running rampant. There are protests and riots in the streets, fights are breaking out between those who are for and against the wearing of facemasks, and the national mood feels so toxic, many people just want to lock their doors and stay home. I can't help but wonder just what effect all of that negative energy might have had on the spirits of the Villisca Axe Murder House.

I'll find out for sure later tonight.

My first stop is to pick up Sarah. I spend a few hours crashed out on the floor in her basement, while she works from home. As a dental professional with a background in epidemiology, plus a love for the paranormal that equals my own, she's a real asset to any investigation I've ever worked on with her.

Sarah and I arrive in Villisca a little before four o'clock in the afternoon. As we turn onto East Second Street, we're met by a striking sight. There, in the middle of the road, is a man on a motorcycle. Bearded, muscled, and tattooed, his eyes obscured by Ray Bans, it can only be the most American human being I've ever met: Johnny Houser. He seems lost in thought, and it seems like a shame to disturb him.

The house sits atop a small, grassy hill. Off to the right is a large barn. I pull into a parking spot outside the house and we hop out. Hugs are off the menu, thanks to the current pandemic, but he's still every bit the same friendly Johnny he always was.

After saying hello, we head for the barn so that I can fill out some paperwork and officially sign for the house. Johnny tells us that the house feels strange again today. He was hoping for a quiet day, but as things turned out, he ended up showing over thirty visitors around on tours before closing up shop at half-past three.

I sign on the dotted line and Johnny, who's standing behind a hanging sheet of transparent Perspex in order to prevent transmission of airborne droplets, tucks the paperwork away in a drawer.

"Good luck," he smiles, in a way that implies we might need it.

Waving goodbye to Johnny, we head over to the house. I unlock the screen door and push the kitchen door open. The house truly is a place out of time. Sarah is right on my heels. We walk from room to room, just acquainting ourselves with the house.

"It does feel weird in here," Sarah says, once we reach the children's bedroom upstairs.

"Weird how?"

"Weird heavy. Weird oppressive."

Personally, I don't feel anything like that myself, but I file it away as being potentially interesting information. We bring in all of our gear, several cases worth, and set it out carefully on the floor of the parlor. It's already gloomy inside the house, and trending rapidly towards darkness as night begins to fall.

Even though it's a bright, sunny afternoon, the interior is dark and drab. We're standing in the kitchen. The floor is mostly hardwood, and creaks a little whenever one of us takes a step. The walls are painted green. The cabinetry and furniture looks to be period-appropriate for the early 1900s, being aged and weathered. There's an iron-top range, atop which sits a chipped iron tea kettle alongside two glass salt-and-pepper shakers. Next to a gas lamp is a mirror, covered with a towel, just as other reflective surfaces were covered by the killer on the night of June 9/10, 1912.

Against one wall is a table that is laid with an assortment of bowls, a milk jug, and cutlery. Mounted on the wall above it is an antique telephone. When it comes to recreating the details of the time, no effort has been spared. Although these items didn't actually belong to the Moores, they are nonetheless very evocative, helping one appreciate what it must have felt like to live in the house back in 1912. Darwin and Martha Linn, presumably with some help from their friends, put a lot of work into restoring the home to some semblance of its original state, and it shows.

Now that the outside door has closed behind us, it's hard to shake the feeling of having been transported back in time a hundred years or so. Everything inside the house is handled with care, not just because some of it is delicate, but rather, because the atmosphere feels hushed and solemn. I'm not remotely sensitive to such things, but after being inside the Moore house for less than a minute, even I can tell that something doesn't feel quite right.

The most obvious explanation for this is, of course, that having researched the history of both the house and the haunting, I've already been influenced to feel that way. I'm going to have to watch my biases when it comes to investigating this house.

Sarah knows the layout well, and gives me the guided tour. Our first stop is the parlor, which today would be called the living room. This would have been the room in which the Moore family spent much of their time. It's directly connected to the kitchen.

Framed monochrome photographs of the Moores adorn the walls and surfaces. I stand there for a moment, just looking at them. None are smiling, as was the custom in those days. It sinks in that those faces which are looking back out at me across the gulf of a century not only lived inside these same four walls, but also spent the last night of their lives here, until they were brutally cut short in the early morning hours.

An upright piano stands against one wall. Heavy drapes are doing a great job at helping keep the parlor dark and cool.

There's a couch and several wooden chairs, situated around a large cast-iron stove. It would feel very homely and comfortable, if one didn't know what had once taken place in the house.

I follow Sarah past the stove into the one ground floor bedroom. The walls have been painted in muted blue tones. The only functioning electrical device in the entire house is bolted into the wall beneath the window, a compact air conditioning unit that hums softly.

The bed, a chest of drawers, and a small closet at the back of the room are all covered with toys and dolls, presumably left as offerings to Lena and Ina Stillinger, who were sleeping in here when the killer came in. Just the thought of what happened in this room is nauseating.

"Show me the upstairs," I ask. Sarah obliges, retracing her steps and going back into the kitchen in order to reach the stairs. The staircase is narrow and each tread creaks and groans no matter where we place our feet. One thing that has puzzled students of the case is the question of how Josiah and Sarah Moore were taken by surprise if the killer had come into the house after dark and climbed up to the second floor. It's already obvious that there's no way to be stealthy on this particular staircase, but with the two Stillinger girls sleeping over, it would have been reasonable for them to have assumed that any footsteps they might have heard belonged to Lena or Ina.

The top of the staircase opens directly onto the master bedroom, at the foot of the bed itself. The double bed is not the one in which Mr. and Mrs. Moore were killed, thankfully, but it is positioned in exactly the same spot. Next to the bed is a vanity table with a large mirror. A faded white sheet has been draped over the glass, preventing any occupant of the house from seeing their own reflection.

Sarah is standing off to the side of the bed, and I realize that it's exactly the same spot in which the killer must have stood when he murdered Josiah Moore. It gives me a sick feeling in the pit of my stomach.

Continuing for just a few steps along the narrow hallway, I come to a wooden door on the left. It has been left ajar, so I open it a little wider and look inside. This is the infamous attic. There are two Amityville-style windows overlooking the street outside. Sitting on the bare floorboards in the middle of the room is a wooden chair. The doorway itself is surprisingly narrow, particularly for a chap like me who's no stranger to the drive-thru, but I squeeze inside. I have to duck in order to avoid hitting my head on the rafters, something which becomes vitally important for me to remember when I notice that the roof is riddled with rusty iron nails. Impaling my head on a few of those won't be any fun, and I can't remember the last time I got a tetanus booster.

The last room in the house is the children's bedroom. I recognize it instantly from the TV, particularly the closet with the door that likes to open itself. It's full of teddy bears, dolls, and plastic balls. I find it endearing that so many visitors have wanted to leave the spirits of the children something to play with. However, I think it's a huge leap to assume that any of the murder victims still haunt the old Moore house, and the same goes for the killer himself. My primary goal in investigating here is to try and get to the bottom of the mystery which surrounds the place. Is it actually haunted at all, and if so who — or *what* — is behind it all?

It's time for us to get to work.

I ask Sarah what she'd like to try first. She tells me that she's never visited the town cemetery before, and would appreciate the opportunity to pay her respects to the Moores and to the Stillingers. Although it isn't far, storm clouds are starting to gather, and so we elect to drive, just for safety. I lock up the house and off we go, but before we leave, I set up a quick control object experiment in the Stillinger girls' bedroom downstairs. There is a small pile of Scrabble letters on top of the dresser next to the bed. I arrange six of the letters carefully to spell out a word. Will anybody be tempted to play around with them while we're gone?

The cemetery is accessed via a narrow gravel road. Sarah and I approach the headstones of Josiah, Sara, and their children first. There is currently a national coin shortage in effect, and many stores are asking customers to supply exact change, which makes it seem all the stranger that so many coins of various different denominations are stacked upon the graves of Josiah and his family, left there by visitors from far and wide. There's also a multitude of small toys and other nick-knacks, primarily on the headstones of the children.

I stand back and let Sarah be alone with her thoughts. When she's done, she takes a couple of photographs and we return to the car. We make it back to the house before it is fully dark. I head straight into the downstairs bedroom and check the dresser. None of the Scrabble letters have been touched. *Oh well,* I tell myself, *nothing ventured, nothing gained.*

Sarah has also brought a couple of her own Scrabble sets with her, and so we decide to broaden our experiment. She places one on the bed in the downstairs bedroom, and spells out a number of meaningful words with the letters: Lena, Boyd, Katherine, Sara, Ina, Herman, Paul, and Josiah (we've run out of letter Hs so have to substitute a blank tile for this last).

Once the first board has been set up, we head upstairs to

the attic. A number of visitors have reported negative experiences in the attic, the part of the house in which some people believe the killer may have hid prior to the murders. Shuffling in on our hands and knees to avoid the low-pitched roof, we put the second board in the center of the room. This time, the words are very different in nature: Axe, Reverend, Killer, Blood, Murder, Attic, Villisca, and Mirror.

We take photographs of each board from multiple angles to use as a reference later on, in case it looks like some of the letters have been moved or manipulated. Then I hammer the flat of my fist into the floorboards several times at varying strengths, sending a series of booming thuds echoing throughout the house. I'm not being dramatic; the intent is to figure out how much vibration it will take in order to move the letters, so we can rule out the possibility of our own footsteps being responsible (doubtful) or even the traffic on the street outside (even more doubtful). We finally conclude that nothing less than a full-power slam on the floorboards will make those letters budge.

The boards will be left in place until tomorrow morning, to give any entities in the house ample opportunity to play around with them.

Our next stop is the children's bedroom upstairs, where the four Moore Children slept. Sarah and I each stretch out on one of the different beds that are pushed against the walls. We discuss the possible identity of the killer, and whether or not he was hiding within the house or broke in after the family had gone to sleep.

Sarah tries to coax the closet door into opening by itself, which it stubbornly refuses to do. The atmosphere inside the house feels calm, almost flat, even to a non-sensitive like myself. Neither of us is remotely on edge, and I could quite easily close my eyes and go to sleep, no matter how fearsome the reputation of this house has become.

As our resident photographer, Sarah has a new camera rig that she's just itching to try. It's a combination ultraviolet (UV) and infra-red (IR) setup, and is triggered either by vibrations that a sensor detects, or an increase or decrease in the IR spectrum. That makes it a "set it and forget it" solution, and Sarah elects to use it in the Stillinger girls'bedroom downstairs. While I sit back and take notes, she begins fussing with a tripod and several lights, flooding the room with a neon-purplish hue. On the walls behind the children's bed, long, dark streaks look like massive hemorrhagic blood stains. The truth, however, is much more palatable: the streaks are nothing more than the residual after-effects of humidity, condensing and dripping down over the course of many years.

Her job now done, she backs slowly away, and we go to the kitchen to enjoy a well-earned cup of tea.

We break out a talking board — in this case, it's an actual Hasbro-brand Ouija Board — and set it up in the master bedroom. Sarah and I wedge ourselves into place beside the bed (the bed itself is too rickety to bear any weight) and she opens up the board with an admonition that only good, honest spirits are permitted to communicate with us through it. Negative, dishonest entities are expressly forbidden to use the board.

The planchette flatly refuses to move, no matter how much we cajole, coax, and try our best to encourage communication. We both get a scare when a loud male voice with an English accent suddenly booms out, "Sorry, I can't find that." It's so close to my ear that I damn near jump out of my skin. When my heart rate finally begins to slow down, it soon becomes clear that there's a perfectly rational explanation: Sarah has forgotten to switch her Siri off. She finds my dramatic over-reaction hysterically funny. I, on the other hand, am just happy to have avoided an unexpected gastro-intestinal emergency, if you take my meaning.

As we're trying to get some kind of conversation going via the board, we both hear a sound downstairs that sounds a lot like a single footstep on the floorboards. Sarah and I exchange a look and head on down. All is in place on the ground floor, and there's nothing obvious to account for the sound.

Next, Sarah and I spend some time in the Moore children's bedroom. Sarah's lounging on one of the beds, while I'm sitting on the floor, running a digital voice recorder as she uses an app on her phone that some people believe allows spirits to communicate with the living. If that is indeed the case (and I'm not convinced that it is) then apparently nobody's interested in talking to us tonight, because the thing isn't giving us anything of value at all.

I'm sitting there, quietly staring off into the hallway that leads to the master bedroom, watching a balloon tied to the arm of a rocking chair drift slowly back and forth near the ceiling. Suddenly, there's a groaning twang from somewhere off to our left. Our heads both snap to look in that direction. Neither of us can see anything unusual, but we can clearly hear the sound of the springs on the bed directly opposite us screeching as if somebody is slowly sitting down on the mattress.

I look at Sarah. Sarah looks at me. Our expressions both say: *You're hearing that too, right?*

Then the sound is repeated, but this time in reverse. It sounds as though the pressure on the springs is being released, as it would be if the invisible sitter was beginning to stand up.

"Well, shit," is the only thing I can find to say. We both get to our feet and walk across the room, in order to examine the bed. There don't seem to be any cold spots or other anomalies on or around it, and the bed has been quiet all night so far.

So, what on Earth had just sat down there in front of us? Neither of us has the foggiest idea.

A thorough checking-over of the bed reveals nothing out of the ordinary that could explain the noises. It hasn't made a sound since we first got here, and doesn't make one for the rest of the night. There's no reason for the springs to have moved that we can determine.

Not conclusively paranormal, but interesting nonetheless.

We spend the next few hours employing various different methods and techniques in an attempt to make contact with whatever haunts the house. Nothing seems to be working. Talking it over, we debate whether the fact that there are just two of us present tonight has provided too little energy for them to draw upon. Perhaps we're starving them of energy. Either that, or maybe they just don't like us...or maybe nothing's here at all.

It's just past three o'clock in the morning. We're sitting in the parlor, taking a five-minute break, when Sarah notices a set of headlights outside the house. I go over to the window and move the curtain aside. There's a pickup truck sitting directly behind mine, engine idling, high-beams glaring into the windows. It sits there for five minutes. Nobody gets out.

Then it drives off, circles the block, and comes back around to do exactly the same thing.

"Who do you think it is?" Sarah wonders.

"I've got no idea. I doubt it's somebody local. They're all tucked up in bed at this hour."

"And the bars should have closed hours ago," she adds.

Five minutes later, the exact same thing happens again. The same pickup truck parks outside the house and simply watches us. The driver and passenger, whoever they are, can clearly see the glow from the Coleman lantern that we're using to light up the kitchen, and my own vehicle is parked outside the house. They know somebody's in here.

Who are they, and what do they want?

If this had happened at a more decent hour, I'd have written it off as being nothing more than a couple of sightseers, out for a drive to check out the infamous Axe Murder House. But who does that at 3.a.m?

Is somebody trying to scare us? If so, to what end? I make myself plainly visible in the window, my head and shoulders backlit by the light from the lantern. They have to realize that we're watching them, watching us. What sort of game are they playing?

Fifteen minutes into this bizarre standoff, Sarah and I are both starting to feel more than a little uncomfortable. We start weighing our options. We could call 911, and while it might seem pretty foolish to get the cops over here in the middle of the night over something as simple as a truck driver behaving strangely, it's actually starting to seem like a good idea. We don't have any other means of protecting ourselves. Generally speaking, bringing weapons into the Villisca Axe Murder House has proven to be a very bad idea in the past. I did bring a fire axe along with me, with the intention of using it as a trigger object. Its presence would be a great deal more reassuring if it wasn't locked up in the flatbed of my own truck, sitting right out there in the street.

Besides, this is rural Iowa. Almost everybody is armed with a weapon of some sort. Knives are common, as are handguns, rifles, and shotguns. If our mysterious nocturnal visitors truly do mean us harm, they've probably come equipped for just that purpose.

Then it hits me: I can call Johnny Houser. He lives just a stone's throw away. I pull out my phone and key in the unlock code, ready to bring up his number. Suddenly, the truck disappears with a squeal of tires, roaring off into the night — and probably waking up half the neighborhood in the process.

Sarah and I breathe a sigh of relief. Hopefully, whoever it was got what they came for and won't be back tonight. Still, we're going to spend the rest of the investigation looking over our shoulder, just in case. Our night at the Moore House has given us a serious case of the creeps alright, but not for the reasons we expected.

The atmosphere still feels disappointingly flat. It also feels like the equivalent of being baked alive in an oven. Every time one of us steps outside to go to the restroom, however, we're reminded of just how muggy and humid this Iowa summer night is. It hits you like a wall the minute you go onto the porch, and it's a relief to get back inside the house again. My clothes are sticking to my skin and I'm starting to feel a little gross.

We've spent the majority of the evening with the air conditioning switched off. Now, Sarah and I are both ready to admit defeat. By mutual agreement, we fire up both AC units. The sense of relief I feel when the chilled air hits my skin is almost palpable.

Back in the parlor, Sarah and I settle into armchairs and try a burst EVP session, again with no results. It's frustrating, but also par for the course when investigating any haunted location. Some nights, no matter how hard you try, you just don't get anything. Although we've had a couple of odd occurrences, such as the camera acting strangely in the Stillinger girls' bedroom, and the bed springs popping for no apparent reason, so far, it's been pretty much a bust.

Some initial puzzlement at what sounded like footsteps is easily debunked by Sarah, who figures out that the drainage water from the air conditioner mounted to the exterior wall upstairs is dripping down on top of the downstairs unit, making a metallic rap-rap-rap that clangs and echoes weirdly throughout the house. We confirm it by switching the upstairs unit off. The sound immediately stops.

We've worked together long enough by now to pretty much know what the other one is thinking. With sunrise fast approaching, we agree that it's time to call it a night. We've thrown almost every trick in the book at the house tonight, and gotten a very minimal return. The key word, however, is *almost.*

"We'll hit it hard tomorrow night," Sarah says. She's right. Sometimes the right thing to do is to cut your losses, go away, and refresh yourself, in the hope of coming back stronger the next time.

It takes us half an hour to bundle up all of our equipment and pack it away, then load it into the truck. We're distracted by a pair of collarless cats who come by to say hello. One is orange with forward-swept ears. It jumps up onto the flatbed of my truck, and meows insistently for my attention. When I scratch its tummy, the cat purrs and licks my hand.

The second cat is dusky gray in color. I instantly name him Mr. Gray. We find him stretched out on the wooden railing outside the barn, apparently interested in doing nothing more than watching the world go by. The cat magnanimously deigns to let me pet him.

After checking the reference photographs for comparison, we're disappointed to see that none of the letters on the Scrabble boards have been interfered with in any way.

For other investigators, the house has been so much more active. Why was tonight such a dud? Is it just one of those things — wrong people, wrong place, wrong time? — or is there something more to it? As I put the truck into reverse and back out slowly into the street, I resolve that tonight, we will go the extra mile.

Well, night two is going to be different...or so I tell myself.

CHAPTER SIX
The Axe

It's four o'clock in the afternoon on our second day, and the air is obnoxiously hot, without even the merest suggestion of a cooling breeze. Inside the Villisca Axe Murder House, it feels still and oppressive, which I suspect has little to do with the weather. The instant we enter the house, Sarah and I make a bee-line for the air conditioning units and switch them on. The blessed relief comes immediately.

We take a slow, methodical walk around the interior of the house, taking in the ambience and making sure that we have no human (or animal) visitors to contend with. From the look on Sarah's face, I can tell she thinks that it doesn't feel any more active than it did yesterday. It's as if the place is in hibernation, just waiting for the right time to wake up. The question remains, is tonight the right time – and are we the right people?

A number of flies seem to have gotten into the house since yesterday. The bloody things are everywhere, zipping past our faces, landing on our arms, and generally making a nuisance of themselves. They're turning out to be most unwelcome house guests.

More welcome by far is Mr. Gray, the cat we befriended last night. He struts up to the back door of the house, acting like he owns the place, and begins to meow. I share a little of my lunch with him, and the cat flops down contentedly on the deck and begins to clean itself. I'm already old news, it would seem.

Sarah sits down in one of the comfortable leather-bound chairs in the parlor, flips open her laptop, and begins clicking her way through some of the photographs she took yesterday.

I, on the other hand, head on over to the barn to answer the call of nature. When I'm finished washing and sanitizing my hands, I head back to the house and find her looking distinctly puzzled.

"You didn't come back inside before now, did you?"

I shake my head, no.

"Huh. Because I just heard the sound of footsteps upstairs."

My ears perk up at that. "How many?"

"Three. Directly above me." That would place them in the Moore children's bedroom. "And that's not all. There was a loud bang, like something was dropped. Based on where I was sitting, it had to have come from inside the attic."

"Then what are we waiting for?" I make for the staircase, but Sarah beats me to it. Our first stop is the attic. Not an object is out of place, from what we can see.

"Are you up here?" Sarah asks. "Do you want to play with us?"

There is, of course, no answer. We retrace our steps and go back through to the children's bedroom. Despite there having been tours of the house throughout the day, it looks much the same as it did last night, and nothing seems to have moved since our initial walkthrough — with one glaring exception.

"Hey, look at this," Sarah breaks my train of thought, pointing at the closet door. I do a double-take.

The closet door is standing wide open.

It was closed when we left the room a short while earlier. Even with the AC running, there isn't enough air flow to open it. It stayed shut throughout our entire investigation the night before, even with Sarah and I stomping around the house creating vibrations on the wooden floors.

But now, there it is. Somehow, the door has managed to open itself.

"Hello?" I call out, a little awkwardly. "Who was running around up here earlier? Who opened the closet door?"

Silence.

We turn our attention back to the bang that Sarah heard coming from the attic. I can't see an obvious way to debunk it. Our first thought was that one of the toys or objects in the attic could have fallen over, but all of them were sitting upright exactly where they had been left. Perhaps one of them had been lifted and dropped somehow?

To test this theory, Sarah goes back downstairs to the parlor and takes up her original seat.

"Okay, I'm ready," she hollers. The air vent in the parlor ceiling, which opens up onto the floor of the children's bedroom, carries the sound of her voice easily. I'm crouching in the attic, sweltering in the hot, enclosed space. The air conditioning doesn't even touch this part of the house, probably because it's at a ninety-degree angle to the main path of air flow, and also because the opening is a small and narrow one.

I pick up the closest object to hand, a toy police car, and drop it from a height of two feet. It clatters on the bare floorboard.

"No, that's not it," Sarah calls back.

I reach for a toy ball, and drop that from the same height. It hits, bounces four times, and rolls.

"A little closer, but not loud enough and there weren't any echoes."

For my third attempt, I select a multi-colored ball with a little more weight to it. It's covered in blunted spikes, causing it to look a little bit like a psychedelic hedgehog. Once again, I let it fall from two feet high.

"That's it!" Sarah yells excitedly. "That's what I heard! Or it's close enough for government work, anyway."

I go back downstairs, glad to be out of the sweatbox.

Cracking open a cold soda, I take a seat opposite her and we discuss the implications of what she had just heard. The closet door opening itself; the sound of three footsteps in the children's bedroom; and lastly, a dull, percussive thud coming from somewhere inside the attic.

It isn't lost on me that all of this occurred while Sarah was on her own inside the house. Did something wait until we were separated in order to start manifesting? If so, then the implications of that are a little disturbing. But for now, Sarah and I are happy. The sun is still up, and things are already more active than they were yesterday. That provides us with some cause for optimism.

After browsing various online articles, forums, and social media posts, it's clear that a number of people have a real problem with paranormal investigators spending time at the Villisca Axe Murder House. I can absolutely see and respect their point.

What happened to the Moore family and to the Stillinger girls in this house was a tragedy. It was also an obscenity. Yet a number of similar axe murders were committed across the United States around that same time period, murders that you are unlikely to hear about other than in the pages of history books. Some took place very close to where I live, in

Colorado Springs. I'd never heard of them until I began researching the Villisca case.

Some have raised the question of whether operating the house as a tourist attraction, inviting the curious visitor and would-be paranormal investigator to tour the house, is in good taste. It is, of course, a matter of personal opinion, and for what it's worth, here's mine.

When Darwin Linn restored the house (presumably at no small expense) he preserved the historic location, so that future generations can visit and experience it for themselves. This not only provides a window into life in early 20th century Villisca, but also helps keep alive the memory of not just the Moore family, but also Lena and Ina Stillinger. Yes, the facts of the matter are macabre and grisly, of that there can be no question; but I would argue that as it stands today, the Villisca Axe Murder House is a piece of living history, and once it is gone, it can never be replaced.

Then we come to the question of ghosts. Some people simply don't believe in them. Quoted in a 2014 article on Vice.com written by Josiah Hesse, documentary film-maker Kelly Rundle said:

The first paranormal investigators visited the house in 1999; they declared the house was haunted, and that they would identify who the killer was.

Despite some of them having made claims to the contrary, no information has ever been obtained (via paranormal means or otherwise) which definitively identifies the killer. No matter what psychics and paranormal investigators may have said, the specific events of June 9 and 10, 1912, are still a matter of conjecture.

Kelly Rundle adds that despite his having spent a lot of time shooting footage inside the house, he didn't experience anything out of the ordinary, and nor did any of the former tenants that he spoke to. (He must not have spoken to the ladies who were interviewed by Zak Bagans for *Ghost Adventures*). Mr. Rundle has raised a very valid point. It's difficult to find many accounts of the house being haunted that date back to before the late 1990s. That doesn't necessarily mean that there weren't any, however.

We must also consider the possibility that whatever haunts the house lay essentially dormant until Darwin Linn purchased and restored it. It is a commonly-accepted belief in the paranormal field that renovation — whether construction or deconstruction — can be a trigger for a haunting to emerge from hibernation, or if it has already been somewhat active, to further grow in intensity. We will explore this concept in more depth as the book progresses.

While I do respect the right of people to believe that investigating a murder scene is in poor form, I obviously do not share that view myself. In the past, I have been fortunate enough to investigate Fox Hollow Farm, home of the serial killer Herb Baumeister, who was known as the I-70

Strangler. Baumeister killed multiple victims at Fox Hollow, most of them in the swimming pool located down in the basement, and disposed of their remains in the woods behind the farm. Fox Hollow is now a private family residence, and the owners have experienced many strange occurrences there. Despite the grisly history of the location, I still believe that it was appropriate for me to delve into the mystery of the haunting. Simply ignoring paranormal phenomena does not make it go away.

I hold the same belief where the Moore House is concerned. The tragic back story should not, I am convinced, deter decent investigators from conducting research into the claims of paranormal activity there. That research should be carried out respectfully, however. Provoking, yelling, screaming, and puffing up one's chest would be poor form, and not the sort of behavior I would either advocate or engage in at a place like Villisca.

With that being said, I am not beyond using suitable trigger objects in an attempt to stimulate paranormal activity. To that end, I go out to my truck and fetch the flat-headed fire axe that I've brought along for just this purpose. Stepping back into the house, I lean the implement head-down against one of the parlor walls. I'm hoping that the dynamic in the environment might subtly change because of its presence. We shall have to wait and see.

"What do you want to try next?" Sarah asks. I tap the

handle of the axe.

"Now that I've brought this into the house, I want to see if anything is triggered by it. Why don't we switch off the air conditioning and sit quietly, run an EVP session?"

"Sure thing. Why don't we separate? You take one floor and I'll take the other?"

That's a great idea. Sarah settles herself into a chair in the Stillinger bedroom downstairs, while I head on up to the Moore children's room. With the AC off, the entire house is silent. There aren't even any pops or creaks as the structure settles after a long, hot day.

I sit myself down in a spot with a good view of the closet and wait, placing a digital voice recorder on the floor next to me. For twenty minutes, nothing happens. Traffic hums quietly by in the street outside, and I can hear the crickets chirruping, but within the house itself, nothing at all.

Playing the audio recording back, I listen to the past twenty minutes all over again. There are no EVPs, no anomalous voices or sounds that I can hear. I go downstairs to check in with Sarah, who has experienced exactly the same thing. Zilch. Zip. Nada.

Letting out a frustrated sigh, I take my electric tea kettle out to the barn in order to fill it up with water. My friends, the stray cats, are back. I give both Ginger and Mr. Gray a small piece of chicken and scratch their tummies. It's dark outside by now. I stand on the lawn between the barn and the house, just looking up at the night sky. Villisca is rural enough that light pollution from the closest big city, Omaha, doesn't affect the view. There's also little in the way of moonlight. The Milky Way arches high above me, a speckled band of stars. Even my home in the foothills of the Rocky Mountains can't match Villisca for its view of the night sky, and I lose track of the time, just staring up into infinity and taking it all in. It makes all of our earthly business seem so small and inconsequential.

After a while — I don't know exactly how long — Sarah emerges from the house. She's a skilled photographer, and has a real passion for astrophotography. Never one to miss out on an opportunity, she is soon laying back on the grass and taking pictures of the heavens above us. I sit and watch, stroking my two feline friends, who purr contentedly and brush themselves back and forth against my ankles. It's a welcome break, and when she has a digital folder full of photographs, we head back indoors for a cup of tea and to plan the next step in our investigation.

We decide to try using a talking board up in the attic. I bring the board and planchette, while Sarah carries the axe. As she reaches the top of the stairs, I notice that there's a slightly faraway look on her face.

"Are you okay?" I ask her. I can't help but let my gaze drift down to her hands, which are holding the axe loosely at her waist.

"It's strange," she says, narrowing her eyes as though trying to work something out. "As I was climbing the stairs just now, I felt...it felt as if there were eyes watching me, and that whoever was watching really didn't approve of *this.*" She gives the axe a couple of shakes for emphasis.

"I can see why they wouldn't. Are you *sure* you're okay?"

"I'm fine." She's all business again. Sarah is one of the toughest, most resourceful women I know. Still, I resolve to keep a close eye on her for the rest of the night, just to be certain that she really is alright. Bending over at the waist, she ducks into the attic, taking the axe along with her. I'm right behind her, getting down onto my knees and laying the talking board out on the floorboards. She sets the axe down in front of the windows with an audible thud.

We're about to engage in something that may be a little unwise. Typically, when we conduct a session with a Ouija board, we emphasize the fact that we're only willing to communicate with good, decent entities, those who mean us no ill-will. Negative and evil spirits need not apply. We took this approach last night, and as a result, the board flatly refused to work. Even so, we made a point of closing the board down safely, which is our standard operating procedure. We've heard too many stories of people who have taken this aspect of using a spirit board lightly, and had some very unpleasant experiences as a result. I'm not sure how many of those stories I believe, but I'm not one for taking chances when it comes to stuff like this.

This time, we open up the board and stipulate that we will communicate with *any* entity that is willing to do so, but stress that we will only allow this for the duration of one single, very short session. Sarah and I are both lying on our bellies, each with two fingers on the planchette.

Once again, it flatly refuses to move an inch. We try for ten minutes, and still get nothing. Exasperated, we close the board, locking it down tight and ensuring that nothing can come through it.

The sound of an engine idling tells us that a car has just stopped outside. Sarah peers out through the attic windows, which look very similar to those iconic, eye-like from the infamous Amityville house. A car full of people look back up at her. She waves and smiles to the kids in the back seat. Then the car pulls away, their curiosity apparently sated.

"More satisfied customers," I smile. Sarah grins. The house has attracted quite a bit of attention while we've been here. Several people have stopped in the street outside, often just standing there and looking up, as though searching the windows for a glimpse of the ghosts that are said to haunt it. One chap stands there for a good fifteen minutes, a slack-jawed expression on his face, before moving twenty feet further up the street and repeating the same process again. We keep a watchful eye on him, and try not to be unnerved. I can't help but think of the stories of Reverend George Kelly having behaved in a similar way on the night of the murders, when he claimed to have been drawn to the house by the voice of God.

I set up a Tesla Coil in the doorway of the downstairs bedroom, hooking it into a *long* power extension cable. This device is composed of a thin metal arm, which spins about a central pivot, and is based on the principle of electromagnetic induction and variations in an electromagnetic field about a central coil. As the arm spins, gaining momentum, two tiny glowing jets of blue plasma flare out of either end. In the darkness of the parlor, the coil creates a flashing circle of actinic electric light, looking like the rotor blades of a helicopter cutting their way through heavily-ionized air.

The Tesla Coil looks spectacular, but that isn't its primary purpose (although Sarah and I hope that the cool light show might attract any child spirits who may be around). Our main goal is to provide a kick of extra energy for such spirits to use in order to help them manifest.

Once again, one of our tried and tested methods of experimentation has failed to work for us here. We clearly need a new approach, and in order to do that, I'm bringing in an old friend to provide some guidance.

I've arranged for a good pal of mine to call me in just a few minutes' time. Stephen is a very seasoned paranormal investigator, in addition to being a priest of the Sacred Order of Saint Michael and a world-class musician. I've worked with him on numerous cases over the years, and he has intuitive capabilities that have proven to be, by and large, rather useful.

"Hey there!" The priest's cheerful voice fills the parlor. It's so good to hear the sound of his voice again. We haven't seen each other for a while, and we spend a few moments catching up before Stephen gets down to business. I'm extremely interested in what, if anything, he can pick up remotely from inside the house. "The room that feels thickest to me right now is the bedroom on the ground floor."

Sarah and I both turn to look at the doorway into the Stillinger sisters' bedroom, where the Tesla Coil is still spinning merrily away about its central axis. Could that be contributing to whatever it is that Stephen is sensing? We can but hope. He assures me that he isn't picking up on the energies generated by the coil itself; to him, Stephen explains, he perceives the energy coming from an electrical device and that of a spirit entity as both having completely different colors.

"What I'm seeing is a kind of blueish mist, and it's isolated to only that room in the house." He pauses to clear his throat. "There's also something going on upstairs, in the kids' closet. There's a very chatty spirit up there. I would consider doing some EVP work up there."

Sarah and I both nod. Those two particular locations are generally considered to be among the more active parts of the house.

"Stephen, do you have any sense of whether these spirits are children, adults, or even something that isn't human?" I ask.

"This isn't a demon and this isn't a family member," he asserts. "In my opinion, you're dealing with beings that were attracted to that house because of the terrible things that happened there."

"Can I ask a question?" Sarah interjects. "Earlier tonight, I was walking up the stairs. I was carrying an axe. I really felt like I was being...*judged*. Like there were a thousand eyes watching me, all of them thinking, 'What the hell are you doing?' Did that somehow agitate what's here?"

"That's just the energy of the place," Stephen tells her. "Remember that there are spirits there that weren't involved in the murders but were attracted to the area because of them. They know all about the history of the house. When they see things like that — somebody taking an axe up the staircase in the way that the killer did — they do sometimes get freaked out."

"I felt like a kid who was caught with her fingers in the candy jar," she admits.

"Mmm," Stephen grunts, thinking for a moment. "The

attic and the kitchen seem really flat. The living room is…moderate. The staircase and both of the kids' bedrooms feel the most active to me."

I'm taking notes. Stephen's advice has stood me in good stead in the past, and I'm determined to follow it again tonight. I ask Stephen what his thoughts are regarding the presence of the killer's spirit haunting the house.

"He's not there," the priest declares flatly. "I've never sensed him there, not a single time. The only even vaguely similar energy to that of a murderer that I've ever picked up on, was in the loft above the barn. But there's no discernible energy there tonight."

That's an interesting observation. I recall Amy Allan claiming to have perceived a thin, scrawny looking figure in the barn, a man whose sketch looked a lot like Reverend George Kelly. Could this be a coincidence, or was it something more?

The barn isn't the original structure, which dated back to the 1800s. This replacement structure came to the Villisca Axe Murder House around the time of the restoration.

"One other thing," Stephen adds. "You have to make *real* sure that you don't allow any of those spirits to come back from there with you. That would be really bad."

"Do you think there's a good chance of that happening?"

"I do, unless you protect yourself. Use the techniques I taught you." Stephen once showed me a method of mentally visualizing a blinding white light, a sort of primal healing force of goodness, flowing through my body and washing away all negative energies and influences. It's like taking a shower in pure light. I've practiced the technique diligently after visiting some of the world's most haunted places, and, so far — fingers crossed — it has prevented me from taking anything unpleasant back home with me.

"I will. Thank you, my friend."

"*You* need to take special care, because they're really most attracted to you," he continues.

"Me? I find that hard to believe. I mean, I'm not exactly the looker here." It's been said before that I have a great face for the radio. At my side, Sarah is smirking and doing her best to stifle her laughter.

"It's nothing to do with looks," Stephen chuckles, pouring cold water all over my ego. "It has to do with your energy. You're very curious, and it's that curiosity that's really drawing them in. I perceive a kind of aura around you, and it's not *you* putting it out...*they're* putting it around you."

The fact is that I am, indeed, very curious. I'm a storyteller at heart, and I'm here to help tell the story of the Villisca Axe Murder House, so what Stephen's telling me does indeed make sense —but there's another reason that I might be of interest to the spirits of the house.

"One of the prime suspects was English," I point out.

"That's right," he remembers. "And your accent may well be familiar to them. Remember, *protect yourself*...and be charming as Hell."

Stephen has surgery scheduled for the following morning, and so he needs to get some sleep, but not without the caveat that if things start to go bad for us tonight, I'm to call him immediately. He is sometimes able to help offer protection remotely. We both thank him and he signs off, leaving us a little clearer about where to focus our time and attention.

CHAPTER SEVEN
Dedman's Hand

Stephen's advice was very clear and direct: to focus our attention on either the children's bedroom upstairs, or the Stillinger girls' bedroom, which is where we find ourselves sitting right now. I'm perching on a small wooden chair that's situated in the closet doorway, while Sarah sits directly opposite me, next to the single bed which occupies the room.

While I set up recording equipment, she breaks out her personal set of dowsing rods. They have luminous green tips, which makes it easy for us to see them moving in the darkness. As with so many other tools used by paranormal investigators and devotees, dowsing rods are controversial. Dowsing devotees swear by them, but opponents point out that the rods could very well be moving as a response to the ideomotor effect — in other words, they're being guided not by mysterious energies, but the user's own subconscious.

I take the view that they are a tool just like any other, and are usually worth trying out, so long as the investigator keeps an open mind and the results are taken with a healthy grain of salt.

The rods immediately begin to move in Sarah's hands when she calls upon them to do so, the tip of one crossing over the top of the other.

"Move the rods apart if you're a girl, and cross them if you're a boy." They obligingly swing away from one another, signifying that whatever we're communicating with claims to be a girl.

"You're doing a great job," she tells the communicator. "Are you younger than ten years old?" The response suggests that they are older than ten and younger than fifteen. Her next question asks if they are eleven years old. The answer is in the affirmative. I remind Sarah that Lena Stillinger was eleven years old when she was murdered in this very room.

From out in the kitchen, there comes a loud crunch. I'm momentarily startled, but Sarah is unperturbed. "Ice shifting in the cooler," she says. I realize that she's absolutely right. There's nothing remotely paranormal about it.

Another train sounds its horn in the distance, that most Villisca of all sounds. Momentarily distracted, Sarah makes herself get back on track.

"So, you are eleven years old, and a little girl. Did you die in this room?"

No, the rods tell us. I lean forward intently.

"Are you telling us the truth about who and what you are, and how old you are?" I demand. The dowsing rods separate, indicating that whoever or whatever is manipulating them has been lying to us.

I let out a sigh of exasperation.

"Are you playing games with us?" Sarah asks. The response is immediate. *Yes.*

We realize that we've been wasting our time, but decide to press on anyway. "Is this fun for you?"

The rods answer *Yes.*

"Do you play tricks on other people who come here?"

This time, the rods spin sharply in Sarah's hands, indicating *Yes*. Sarah follows up by asking whether the communicator enjoys scaring people, and gets the same answer. This tracks with what a number of people have claimed about there being prankster spirits in the house.

When she asks whether they are *really* a little girl, the rods become suddenly coy and reluctant to move. Until this point, they have been pivoting freely in her loose grip. Now, they're stiff and uncooperative. From my seat inside the closet doorway, I hear a loud creak coming from up above me.

I look up. There's no way *that's* ice cracking in the cooler. The noise was a heavy creak on the staircase.

We go out to check, and of course, there's nothing there. Nothing seems amiss up on the second floor either. Sarah and I take a break, enjoy a hot cup of tea, and get ready to greet our next special guest. The story he is about to share with us is nothing short of terrifying.

Although Chris Dedman hasn't been back to the Villisca Axe Murder House in several years, he is gracious enough to agree to join us by phone. I, for one, am excited to hear the story of his encounter with the dark entity inside the house at first hand, and also to see whether his recounting it will stir up any energies for Sarah and I.

Chris calls me promptly at the agreed-upon time. I put him on speaker, setting my phone down on the floor in the center of the parlor, alongside a digital voice recorder. We exchange greetings. Chris is in fine spirits ("If I was doing any better, I wouldn't be able to stand myself!") and I thank him sincerely for taking the time out to talk to us.

He speaks with a distinctly southern accent. "I'm detectin' a trace of an accent," he tells me, without any hint of irony. "Where are y'all from?"

"I'm from back east," I deadpan, giving him my standard response. "About five thousand miles back east...the United Kingdom."

Chris chuckles. He has an infectious laugh and I find myself warming to him immediately. We all settle down and he begins to tell us his story.

His first visit to the Villisca Axe Murder House was in January of 2008. He was working a paranormal case in Missouri, realized that the drive to Villisca wasn't all that far, and on the spur of the moment decided to cross the infamous location off his bucket list.

When Chris entered the house for the first time, he was surprised to encounter a very strong smell of bacon. It was so strong that he wondered if somebody had actually been cooking bacon just a few minutes before their arrival, despite the fact that the kitchen is no longer functional. Although he had a passing familiarity with the general events surrounding the Villisca Axe Murders, he had not been aware of the fact that the killer was believed to have used some bacon that he found in the kitchen as a means of sexual gratification. Some believe that he may also have eaten some bacon himself after having committed the murders.

One thing is for certain: Johnny Houser (the keyholder at the time) had not been cooking anything in the house that day. In fact, eating food in the house is still against the posted rules to this day.

From his seat in the parlor, Chris had a good view through the doorway into the Stillinger sisters' bedroom. He and his fellow investigator caught frequent glimpses of a shadow figure darting back and forth inside the room. Eerily, the figure was about the height of a young child.

This is when I realize that even as we speak, I'm sitting in the very same spot that Chris was sitting in on that day in 2008. I can't help but stare into the open bedroom doorway. Nothing appears to be stirring in there at the moment.

After some time had passed, Chris and his colleague went upstairs to the second floor. Halfway up the staircase, he felt something tangibly coming down towards him from above. Although he could see nothing, whatever it was had enough force to shove him backward, almost causing him to fall. It was only the presence of his fellow investigator behind him that saved Chris's neck.

"What do you think it was?" I ask, intrigued.

"I think it was a residual thing, the killer leaving the house," Chris says. That's a fascinating idea. Personally, I suspect it's slightly off-base. All indications are that the murderer did not rush out of the house that morning, but rather, that he took his time, even cleaning up first. However, I *do* think it's possible that this could have been a residual imprint of the killer heading downstairs to murder Ina and Lena Stillinger. Assuming that they were killed last — and we will never know for sure — then they represented the victims who were most likely to flee the house and escape. The girls were on the ground floor, after all, and had several windows and doors through which they could have fled. While it makes sense that he would have stolen into the house quietly after breaking in, and then snuck upstairs, or could have quietly moved from bed to bed on the second floor while murdering the entire Moore family, the time for him to have moved quickly would have been after everybody was dead on the second floor, and while the Stillinger sisters were still alive. There is also the fact that the killer took the time to remove the key from the door and lock it behind him.

Chris and his companion heard the screen door slam behind them, as though somebody had just exited. They were the only two people in the house, however, and there was no wind to have caught the door and slammed it.

As their investigation continued, the attic remained quiet throughout. The most active room by far seemed to be the Moore children's room. Chris watched in astonishment as a child's ball rolled across the floor from one bed to another, then suddenly stopped in place. It then reversed course, rolling back to its original starting position. This was far too precise a series of movements to be explained away by a sloping floor (no floor can slope in two opposite directions) or random drafts.

They also saw the closet door apparently moving on its own, something that many visitors to the house have experienced.

"I always approach these things from a place of respect," Chris continues. "This was an early point in my career — I was a *Scooby Doo* investigator, mostly doing cemeteries and places like that. This was the first nationally-known haunted location I had ever investigated."

Chris asked whether there was somebody in the closet, perhaps one of the children, that wanted to play. In response, the door opened a few inches, and then swung shut, as though somebody inside had pulled it closed.

"It's okay to come out," he coaxed. "Are you lonely? It's safe."

The door opened itself again, just wide enough for

somebody to peek out, and then closed itself once more.

Chris and his companion spent the next few minutes trying to debunk what had just happened, ruling out such explanations as freak drafts, old, creaking floorboards, and vibrations caused by stepping on specific parts of the floor. None of it worked.

"In my heart, I'm convinced that we were communicating with one of the dead children that night," he continues. "We didn't get any EVPs, and other than almost getting pushed down the steps, I never felt threatened in the house...not on that first visit. If anything, I felt sorry for the family. I'm a dad, and children died there."

As the months passed, Chris retained his fascination with the Villisca case. He got to know Johnny Houser a little better, and shared his experiences with him. It fell to Johnny to break the unenviable news about what the killer had done with a slab of bacon after the murders.

Time passed. Chris found himself working on a paranormal case in Illinois in which, he says, a young girl was demonically possessed. The case took a heavy emotional toll on everybody involved. As Chris begins to talk about it, three loud beeps indicate that the call has dropped. I look at my phone, puzzled. Four bars. Verizon has served me well in

Villisca so far.

I call him back right away. "This is what happens whenever I talk about this story," Chris tells me. "Let's just say that this is not the first time this has happened. Anyway, back to the case in Illinois..."

The client in this particular case had become convinced that her home was haunted. In an attempt to find out more, she embarked on a series of very lengthy solo EVP sessions. Rather than the standard burst sessions that we typically use, or even longer thirty to forty-five-minute sessions, hers lasted for many hours on end. Before long, the young lady had become obsessed with the possibility that she was the center of a malevolent haunting.

Chris had *thirty-five hours* of raw EVP recordings to listen to when he first took on the case. He says that the client managed to invite a demon into her life. "It ended up being Legion, which is a very *nasty* demon," Chris adds. I'm not sure that if demons truly do exist, there are any which *aren't* nasty, but assume he means that this is one of the worst.

As mentioned earlier, the story of Legion comes to us from the New Testament. Jesus asks a man for his name and is told, *"Legion, for we are many."* The name refers to a host of evil spirits which had taken up residence inside this unfortunate individual. Jesus was said to have cast out the demons, sending them instead into a herd of swine, which promptly stampeded into the sea and drowned.

"For three months, I dealt with this case all by myself," says Chris. "When it first came up, the team I was a member of was very solid. After our first night investigating there, everybody was badly shook up."

Shortly after that, the team disintegrated. Each of the former members experienced some very disturbing events, including serious medical conditions and potentially life-threatening car crashes. At least one member of the team was sitting at home and heard voices telling him to pick up a knife and kill members of his own family with it.

A well-known psychic medium declared that it was one of the worst cases of malevolent evil that he had ever encountered. "I can't believe that this hasn't affected us more."

"Actually, it has," the medium replied. "Something bad is happening to one of you *right now*. And you need to get it taken care of before somebody dies..."

Health issues were plaguing one of Chris's colleagues. Then Chris was affected himself. The results of a recent physical came back, and he was not given a clean bill of health: his heart was larger than normal, something he was really not expecting to hear.

The experience was not a positive one, but it did ultimately strengthen Chris's faith. When he returned to the Villisca Axe Murder House with several friends, the paranormal activity began almost immediately. A Ghost Box radio sweeping device put out the word *Reverend.*

"Reverend who?" Chris asked.

Reverend, the box repeated.

"Reverend *who?*" he pressed.

Reverend Kelly.

He was familiar with Kelly, and his status as a central suspect in the murders. "Reverend Kelly — is that you? Are you here?"

Yes, said the box.

"Is there anybody else here?" There was no response. "Is there anybody here?"

Chris *knew* that somebody was there. Why weren't they talking?

"In the name of Jesus Christ, I command you to tell me your name!"

The Ghost Box said: *Legion.*

The old cliche about blood running cold made itself known right about then. Chris immediately ended the Ghost Box session. All he could think about was getting out of the house. He rushed through the kitchen door and made for the ramp that would take him out to the street.

That's when it hit him.

"It felt as if somebody took a baseball bat and slammed it right across my chest," he recalls. "It knocked the breath right out of me."

Chris stood there, midway down the ramp, clutching his chest and fighting to control himself. Concerned, his teammates gathered around him. *My back feels like it's on fire,* he thought to himself. *Something's very, very wrong...*

He pulled his shirt up in front of everybody, exposing his chest and back. A raised welt on his chest had somehow formed. It was shaped like the letter L.

L for Legion.

As far as Chris was concerned, that was it. There was no way he was going back inside the house for the rest of the night. He was convinced that this haunting was now much deeper and darker than he had ever suspected.

"So, you're saying that this entity — the demon, Legion — followed you from the private help case to Villisca?" I ask.

"I believe that, given the evil events that took place in the Villisca Axe Murder House, plus who knows how many visitors have messed around with seances and Ouija boards in there—" Sarah and I exchange a sideways glance "—I feel that it really did help attract Legion from the case in Illinois. I spoke with Lorraine Warren and John Zaffis, not to mention the priest who was assisting us with the case, and they all said the same thing to me: *You know that you're marked now, right?"*

After receiving his mark on the ramp outside the house, Chris would end up taking a long break from the world of the paranormal. He experienced a great deal of stress and misfortune after his encounter, and is still dealing with some of the after-effects to this day.

"I have to ask, Chris...is it your opinion that this entity, Legion, is still at Villisca, or has it moved on?"

He lets out a long breath. "At first, I thought it had moved on. I did come back briefly, in order to film for *Ghost Adventures*. As soon as I stepped back on the property, I could feel the evil. I could feel the energy being drained out of me, like somebody was tearing out my soul. I refused to go into the house. That's why my interview took place outside.

"There is definitely something still there. Is it Legion? I don't know. Who knows what people have brought along with them, or opened up doorways and allowed to come through?"

I ask Chris about his thoughts toward the Villisca Axe Murder House today.

"I have made my peace with the house," he tells me. "I've been back a couple of times — always during the daytime — but I have not investigated there. There is something sinister there, and it's only a matter of time before it finally shows itself...if it hasn't done so already."

"My advice to anybody who goes into that house is this: I don't care who you pray to, or where your positive energy comes from. Surround yourself and protect yourself with that energy, because if you do not, you may well take something home with you that you do not want."

His words of warning echo those which Stephen offered earlier, and I assure Chris that Sarah and I will take them very seriously. On that note, we thank Chris for his willingness to make an early-morning phone call in order to share his story, and we say goodbye. He was kind enough to offer up prayers for our safety and wellbeing, something for which I am very grateful.

"Well," I say, heading into the kitchen to grab an energy drink. "What do you want to do next?"

Sarah considers for a moment and then says, "I think we should hit the Moore kids' bedroom."

CHAPTER EIGHT
Playing Games

One of the more unusual methods I've picked up over the years is known as the Human Pendulum. Despite the name, it has nothing to do with an actual pendulum; rather, it involves using the body of a willing volunteer as a signaling device, one that will sometimes respond to yes/no questions that are asked of it.

The technique is a controversial one. There are many who believe it is a genuine conduit for spirit communication. On the other hand, skeptics quite rightly point out that the whole thing could be explained away by the ideomotor effect — a type of movement of which the person performing it, is totally unaware is guided by their own subconscious. Whether it's paranormal or not is really up to the individual to decide – at least, until the technique has been rigorously studied in a controlled environment. I've had some very impressive results using this technique over the years, but at the same time, I've also seen it fail utterly.

This is Sarah's first time acting as the Human Pendulum. She finds a clear space to stand in the center of the upstairs children's bedroom. I sit off to her left side, so that I can watch carefully for any indications of bodily movement. Her stance is straight, with her feet slightly less than a shoulder-width apart, and she looks straight ahead, gazing at the closet door.

I clear my throat. "We're about to open up Sarah as a Human Pendulum. If there are any spirits present in this room that are willing and able to communicate with us via this particular medium, please make your presence known by moving Sarah to her *Yes* position."

Sarah is, it's fair to say, quite a low-key individual in terms of her reactions to the paranormal. I don't think I've ever seen anything faze her at a haunted location. Now, there's just the slightest hint of "Wow" on her face as something lifts her off the heels of her feet and pushes her forward.

"That was...*weird,*" she says, still processing what happened. I'm not surprised. I've seen this happen a lot to first-time Pendulums, and have also experienced it myself. When the unexpected movement of your body happens, it causes the most bizarre feeling to surge through your body.

"What did you feel?" I ask her.

"I don't know...I just felt like I *needed* to lean forward. But, it wasn't *me.*"

She's absolutely right. It may have been her own subconscious mind, or an entity of some kind, but either way, she certainly wasn't doing it deliberately. Watching it happen is one of the joys of using this particular method.

"Forward is Sarah's *Yes,*" I say, speaking primarily for the benefit of my voice recorder. "Thank you very much for that. Now, please show us Sarah's *No* position."

Five seconds pass. Then she rocks backward on her heels, as though somebody has taken her by the shoulders and gently pushed.

"Backward is no," I note, rubbing my hands together in satisfaction. "Perfect. Forward is yes, backward is no. Are you alone in here? In other words, are you the only spirit?"

Sarah sways backward, indicating no.

Sarah doesn't speak. She simply goes with the flow, letting whatever force is at work here move her body in response to my questions.

"Did you die in this house?" This is the big one. An affirmative answer will suggest that we're communicating with one of the Moores or the Stillinger girls. The answer is a very clear *No*.

"Thank you for that. Did you come in here with a visitor, attached to them?" *No*. I'm relieved to hear that neither Sarah nor I have brought along an attachment with us.

"Were you drawn to this place because of the murders which happened here in 1912?" There's a very strong *Yes*. Assuming that it's truthful, this would support the theory held by my friend Stephen that this house draws in spirits because of the negative energy that is contained within its walls.

I take a deep breath and ask the question I'm really hoping won't be a *Yes*. "Were you actually *responsible* for those murders?"

The *No* we get is very clear, almost pushing Sarah back off her feet. That's good news.

"Did you come here to try and help in some way?" *Yes.*

Continuing on in the same vein, we learn that the unseen communicator claims to be neither a male nor a female, neither a boy nor a girl...but instead, something that says it isn't human. That earns a raised eyebrow.

"Are you telling us the truth?"

Sarah is pulled forward, indicating that yes, our invisible friend — assuming that's what's really going on here — insists that they are being honest. I'm far from convinced about that, however.

"This is so weird," Sarah says, shaking her head. There's a big grin on her face.

"Do you have good intentions?" I ask, addressing the communicator, not Sarah herself. *Yes,* is the answer, though it's one that we would do well to take with a grain of salt. I always describe talking to so-called spirits, whether it's using a talking board, an EVP session, a Spirit Box, or something like the Human Pendulum, as the paranormal world's equivalent of an Internet chat room. In other words, you have to take the word of somebody you can't see, that they are who they say they are. There's a very good reason for stranger danger to exist. "Are you enjoying talking with Sarah and I?"

Yes.

"Would it be okay if Sarah asked you a question or two?"

The answer, surprisingly, is *No.* That does seem to support Stephen's contention that the attention of the spirits in the house is mostly focused on me, rather than her. She has the good grace not to take it personally.

"It likes *you,*" she snorts.

"Do you prefer talking to me than to Sarah?" *Yes,* comes the answer.

From out in the master bedroom, we hear the sound of something moving. Naturally, when I look, there's nothing there. I ask the Pendulum whether it was responsible for making the noise, which it promptly denies. However, when I ask if it *knows* who made the noise, the response is an immediate *Yes*, though it refuses to tell me who made the noise.

"A cold breeze just came in and hit my feet," Sarah announces.

"Did another spirit just enter the room?" I ask. The Pendulum states that yes, one did. "Is this spirit a friend of yours?" Judging by how forcefully Sarah is moved, the answer is a strong *No.*

"Do you like this other spirit?" No, again, and just as strong. Is there some degree of antagonism or rivalry between the two entities, perhaps? I ask whether the newcomer can be permitted to communicate via Sarah, but permission is refused.

From downstairs, we hear a loud thump. The sound traveled up through the air vent in the floor. Sarah and I exchange a look. This is starting to get interesting.

"Are you *always* in this house?" I enquire. *Yes*, is the answer. "But can you travel to other places?" *Yes.*

I try again to let Sarah ask some questions, but we get yet another refusal. "Do you like Sarah?" I ask, a little exasperated. *No,* comes the answer. "Do you like me?" *Yes.* I'm doing my best to ignore Sarah's mocking I-told-you-so grin.

I should add that to my resume. *Occasionally popular with ghosts.*

Then, just like that, communication stops. There's a loud creak from the attic. Almost as if an off switch has been thrown, the Pendulum stops working. Sarah's hands have begun to tingle in a rather strange way, so perhaps it's time to quit.

"We are now closing Sarah down as a Human Pendulum." I'm talking to thin air, but what I'm saying is no less important for that. "This means that any spirits, entities, or other communicators who have either spoken through her or have attempted to do so, must relinquish their hold on her. None of you may attach to her, stay connected in any way, or attempt to follow us from this place. You are to remain here."

Always wanting to end on a polite note, I then thank whoever it was that elected to communicate with us, and suggest that Sarah sits down before she falls down. Being the Human Pendulum is hard work, and not just because it requires standing still for so long, staring straight ahead into nothingness. There's a strange kind of weariness which often accompanies the technique, although you only tend to notice it once the session is over and you are finally able to relax.

We chill out and chat for a few minutes, then discuss what we want to try next. I'm fully prepared to give the Pendulum a try myself, but Sarah wants another shot at it. I ask specifically for a different communicator this time. Whether that's what we'll actually get is anybody's guess, but once we've established her *Yes* and *No* positions, which are the same as they were before, the answers start coming thick and fast, much stronger this time.

This communicator claims to be different than the one we were just dealing with; rather, it says that it's a female. She denies having lived or worked in this house, claiming instead that she arrived with a visitor and stayed behind once they had gone — in other words, the classic hitch-hiking attachment.

Why, then, did she choose to stay behind? Because she liked the company of the other spirits who were already resident at the house. "I could feel her pushing me before the question was even out of your mouth," Sarah tells me. That's not unusual. With many EVPs, the disembodied voice will deliver an answer part-way through the sentence that contains the question. It's as if the entity with whom we are interacting is able to read our minds, rather than having to wait for us to actually finish forming the words.

"Would you say that there are a lot of spirits in this house?" *Yes.* "Are all of them nice, friendly spirits?" The *No* is a very forceful one. Sarah has to work to recover her balance.

This communicator also claims to be a decent and honorable entity, but unlike her predecessor, the phantom female — if that's really what we're communicating with — consents to having Sarah ask a few questions. It's unusual to have the Pendulum also asking the questions, but I figure any spirits that might be in here with us must surely be sick of hearing my voice by now.

We try to coax the spirit communicator into opening the door for us. The answer is no, which is further explained when we're told that she isn't capable of doing so. She also refuses to make a sound for us elsewhere in the house.

"Do you dislike us asking questions?" *Yes,* comes the answer, but when I clarify by asking whether she finds our questions annoying, we're told that she does not. How strange.

"Do you dislike them because you're worried that we

might find out something that you don't want us to know?" A very strong affirmative response this time. Apparently, she doesn't want us prying into the various goings-on of the house.

I ask whether any of the Moores or Stillingers are still in the house. We're told that they are not, something that I find to be of great comfort.

"Does their killer ever come back to this place?" Surprisingly, the answer is *Yes*. Score one for Brad and Barry Klinge, stars of the TV show *Ghost Lab,* who firmly believe that their EMF detectors captured the passage of the killer as he went from bed to bed. Now that we're on the subject of the murders themselves, I decide to go for broke. "Was there more than one killer?"

Sarah rocks backward, signifying that there was not. That certainly fits with my view of the case. I've always found the "multiple murderers" theory a little too difficult to buy into. It's time to narrow it down even further.

"Was the murderer Reverend George Kelly?"

No.

"Was the killer influenced by something that was already here in the house?" Sarah asks.

No.

"Did the murderer enter Villisca on the train?" I ask.

Yes.

"And did the murderer also *leave* Villisca on the train?"

No.

Now, assuming there's any truth to the statement, this *is* interesting. Bloodhounds followed a trail from this very house, through the streets of Villisca, to the river...where it was lost. That's not to say that the so-called "man from the train" wasn't responsible, just that he had chosen a different method of making his getaway.

"Did the murderer walk out of town on foot?" *Yes.*

I ask whether the killer will ever be identified. This is perhaps the strongest *No* Sarah has received all night, but she does a great job of keeping her balance. I also believe this statement with one hundred percent certainty. There's no way the killer will ever be definitively identified. Too much water has passed under the bridge since the murders were committed, and far too much of the evidence was contaminated by the time the first law enforcement officials even reached the scene.

"Did the murderer travel to a town called Malvern afterward?" I'm disappointed that the answer comes back *No.* "Do you know the identity of the killer?" *No.*

And then...

"Are you answering my questions honestly?"

No.

My face falls.

"Are you playing games with us?"

Yes.

That's when I realize that in our haste to start off the second session, although we asked for a different communicator, I neglected to specify that we would only communicate with decent, honest spirits.

It looks like the trickster is back.

"Is this amusing to you?" I ask, definitely not seeing the funny side of it myself. Sarah feels another cold breeze swirling around her feet and ankles. The air conditioning hasn't been on for hours.

There's no response.

And we're done.

CHAPTER NINE
Asleep

Despite the hot tea and other caffeinated beverages, Sarah and I are running on fumes. It's now three-thirty in the morning and our EVP recordings are going to be filled with yawns.

The Human Pendulum experiment yielded some interesting, but also contradictory results. For at least part of it, we can't help but feel that we got played. It may well have been the same prankster spirit that we encountered in the Stillinger girls' bedroom downstairs. On the plus side, we have no good explanation for the unusual noises that took place during our session, as they weren't typical of the usual settling sounds the house makes after a hot day.

Now we're starting to feel a little ragged around the edges. There's also the fact that Sarah has to be at work by eight-thirty this morning.

We debate packing up and leaving now, but instead, we finally come to the conclusion that neither of us has slept at the house before, and this might be a good opportunity to do one more experiment.

Chris Dedman's warnings are still ringing loud in my ears, and I don't want to just blow them off. At the same time, I have Stephen's assurance that as far as he can tell, there aren't any malevolent entities around tonight. I'm not a big fan of sleeping at haunted locations, particularly those with dark and tragic histories. For one thing, when we fall asleep, we let our guard down. If you're a believer in the concept that we all have some form of natural 'psychic defense mechanism' — and I'm beginning to see it that way — then its' worth considering the theory that when we go to sleep, that particular form of protection is either switched off, or at the very least is significantly weakened.

With that being said, the house hasn't given us a great deal to work with tonight. It may be that rendering ourselves just a little bit vulnerable will draw out whatever is said to haunt the place. Bearing that in mind, we decide that the second-floor children's bedroom is the best place for us to get some shut eye. Sarah chooses a single bed by the window, and I plan to stretch out on the double bed which stands against the wall. Right next to my head is the notorious closet door.

Sarah's too tall for her bed, and looks pretty funny with her feet sticking out through the spokes on the wrought-iron frame.

"Is the downstairs door locked?" I ask her.

"I don't know," she mumbles, closing her eyes.

I have to go and check. It would be stupid to go to sleep without making sure that the house is secure, and while we make a point of locking ourselves in whenever we're inside, it's possible that we could have forgotten to do so the last time we came in from the barn.

Making my way carefully downstairs with a flashlight to guide me, I confirm that the door is indeed locked. On my way back up, I make sure that both air conditioning units are switched off and close both of the doors leading to the attic. Sarah is wide awake when I walk back into the bedroom.

"What?" I ask.

"I heard wind chimes."

"Wind chimes?"

"Yeah. Right after you went downstairs. They sounded pretty close."

There are two sets of wind chimes in the house, to my knowledge. One set is hanging from the ceiling in the closet downstairs, in the bedroom once occupied by the Stillinger girls. The other...I wrack my memory. Then it hits me. I reach out and open the closet door next to my bed. The wind chimes affixed to the back of the door jingle insistently.

There's an entry in the guest book written by some visitors who experienced the same thing — chimes on the back of the closet door in the children's bedroom moving by themselves.

"That's it," Sarah nods. "They were moving. On their own."

"Could it have been the vibration of my feet on the floorboards?" I ask doubtfully. Sarah shakes her head.

"I don't think so. Besides, we've been in and out of this

room lots of times over the past few days, and we haven't heard a peep until now."

She's right. All of my stomping around with my size twelve feet hasn't made the chimes jingle, so why would it spontaneously happen now? Sarah's choice of bed is starting to look a lot less silly to me with every passing second.

Still, I'm a stubborn middle-aged male, and that means I'm too stupid to back down now, no matter what's happening in the closet. I close the door firmly and say, ostensibly to Sarah but actually speaking to anybody else that might be listening, that it would be quite the thing if the closet door happened to open itself before morning. She solemnly agrees, rolls onto her side, and is fast asleep within seconds of her head hitting the pillow.

There's no way I'm going to miss the door spontaneously opening if it happens. I set up an infrared camcorder in front of the window, pointing back toward my bed. Its lens covers not only the closet door, but also the corridor leading to the attic, master bedroom, and the top of the staircase.

Once the record button has been hit, I lay down on the bed and do my best to get comfortable. I have to sleep diagonally, just to prevent my feet from snarling up in the bedframe at the bottom. I switch off the lantern, plunging the room into near-darkness. Some ambient light filters in through the covered windows., but not a whole lot.

I close my eyes and try to clear my mind. It's at this exact point that my bladder reminds me I really ought to have emptied it before going to bed. I'm sleepy enough that I can't be bothered to go all the way out to the barn, so I do my best to ignore the vaguely uncomfortable feeling. I can hear Sarah's breathing change to the soft, rhythmic pattern which is indicative of her drifting off into deep sleep.

Lucky Sarah. My mind obstinately refuses to switch off. As I lay here in the darkness, my subconscious seizes on the opportunity to remind me that this is the exact spot in which one of the poor, unsuspecting Moore children was brutally murdered 108 years ago. I try to force myself to relax, but my overactive imagination is having none of it. It's conjuring up mental images of the attic door opening, then somebody sneaking out of hiding and making his way stealthily along the corridor, axe in hand, to kill his first victim.

Stop it. You're a grown man, and that happened more than a century ago. Stop psyching yourself out.

Or maybe it didn't happen that way at all, some part of my brain gleefully suggests. Now it's painting the picture of a man quietly forcing the door or one of the downstairs windows. He makes his way carefully upstairs, clutching the axe he took from the barn — Josiah Moore's axe. This man is intent on killing everybody who's sleeping inside the house, and he will be successful. Most of them won't even hear their death coming.

Seriously, knock it the hell off!

I'm starting to get angry with myself, pissed off at my own psyche. If that isn't the dumbest way for me to be reacting right now, I don't know what is. So, I consciously force myself to look on the bright side. I'm learning a lesson right here and right now in the tremendous power of suggestion. Years and years of watching countless horror movies, and listening to spine-chilling stories has set me up to be afraid of the dark. No, not the dark...the things that hide in it. The hidden things. The concealed things.

Because that's the great lesson of the Moore House and the Villisca Axe Murders. No matter how often we might tell ourselves that there's nothing to fear, that the monsters we think are lurking in the darkness aren't real...sometimes that's wrong. The events which took place in this bedroom in the early morning hours of June 10, 1912, provide horrific proof of that.

But that was then, and this is now. I'm locked in a mind game against myself. Based upon the sounds of her slow, regular breathing, punctuated by the occasional snore, Sarah isn't the least bit bothered. I'm cursed with the imagination of a writer, which is often a blessing, particularly when it comes to evoking mental images and putting them into words — but for that very same reason, it now feels like more of a curse.

Just how much of the Villisca case is haunting, and how much is something else — folklore, legend, a grisly tale that grew in the telling? That question lies at the very heart of the whole affair, and it's one that I don't feel any closer to being able to answer just yet. With that final thought still at the forefront of my mind, I finally, mercifully, drift off to sleep.

CHAPTER TEN
Thought Form

The strident jangling of the alarm on Sarah's phone wakes us both up. I crack open one sleep-gummed eye. Grey morning sunlight is streaming through the windows. Rolling over to face the center of the room, I see that the closet door is still closed, just as I'd left it the night before.

Bollocks.

Getting slowly up off the bed and blinking myself into some semblance of wakefulness, I peek out into the hallway. All is silent and still. Sarah lets out a yawn which is loud enough to warn off ships caught in a fog bank. I go to check on the attic, and find that both doors are also still closed.

We haven't had any nocturnal visitors.

Our mood is a little subdued as we pack up our equipment and make one last circuit of the house to ensure that we didn't miss anything. Mr. Gray is waiting for me at the back door, meowing loudly, insistent on being fed. I suspect that we're not the first visitors to the Villisca Axe Murder House to be accosted by this feline panhandler, and we certainly won't be the last. He's getting ready to make a run at the door and dart inside. I flip him a piece of chicken left over from my lunch, and he slinks off to chow down on it, seemingly content with his spoils...for now.

Sarah and I pack up all of our gear and load up the truck.

Despite our very best efforts, the house has raised more questions than it has given answers.

The house wasn't nearly as active as we had anticipated, but as Sarah reminds me on the drive back, that's just the nature of the beast sometimes. Spirits aren't performing monkeys. Sometimes they'll show up and interact with you. Sometimes they won't.

And sometimes, they'll surprise you in the most unexpected of ways. My investigation into the haunting of the Villisca Axe Murder House is far from over.

The following evening finds Sarah and I hanging out at one of our favorite haunted locations: Malvern Manor, also in Iowa. I'd written a book about the haunting *(The Devil's Coming to Get Me: The Haunting of Malvern Manor)* and whenever I'm in Iowa, I always make a point of dropping in to visit. I've become rather fond of the old place.

It's not a formal investigation, just a low-key overnight stay. Now, I've gotten some sleep, and am sitting on the couch in the Manor's break room, sipping some tea and writing up a few notes on the events of the past couple of days. My Facebook inbox pings, alerting me to an instant message from an acquaintance. They've noticed that I have been at Villisca, and wanted to make me aware of their friend's take on the case.

That friend was a paranormal investigator named Dawn Biery, and she has written a blog post about the haunting which makes me sit up and pay attention.

She claimed to have encountered the *residual* (emphasis mine) energies of Ina and Lena Stillinger. Residual hauntings are little more than echoes of the past, a form of paranormal recording in which some type of energy we do not yet understand is imprinted upon the environment. This imprint can be detected later by those who are sufficiently attuned and sensitive to that type of energy. Dawn's rationale for the after-echo of the Stillinger girls still being present in the house is that they died while away from their home and family.

I don't find this particularly difficult to believe, but her next comments are what really pique my interest. She claims that there are two

Trickster spirits. These 2 spirits make up for the majority of the paranormal activity being perceived in the location. Yes, they are toying with you.

This immediately resonates with both Sarah and myself. We're thinking back to the human pendulum method of the night before, in which we received several mutually contradictory answers to our questions, and when I finally challenged the communicator, was told that we were being lied to and played around with. That certainly sounded like a "trickster spirit" to me.

Dawn goes on to describe sensing a "shadow mass" in the attic, a negative thought-form that exists somewhere outside of our own dimension. This would basically be an aggregation of extremely negative and toxic energy, which has taken on a somewhat coherent form and is capable of influencing events on our own plane. It may seem like quite an "out there" idea, but it's not completely without precedent.

Thought forms are not a new concept. In fact, as I write these words in the break room at Malvern Manor, a thought form is supposed to "haunt" (if that is the correct word) the second floor, just above where I'm sitting. Her name —*it's* name — is Inez. Inez Gibson was a young girl who, it was claimed, died here at the Manor in 1900. The story goes that a heartbroken Inez was found hanging in an upstairs closet, and now her restless shade walks the halls of Malvern Manor forever.

There's just one small problem. Inez Gibson didn't die here. She died at her home, a private residence located elsewhere in Malvern. It hasn't even been determined whether she actually set foot inside the Manor during her lifetime. Yet before the truth about this was known, the story of Inez supposedly dying up on the second floor was told over and over again inside these walls by people who didn't know any better.

It wasn't long afterward that visiting paranormal enthusiasts began to have interactions via the Spirit Box and collected EVPs from an entity claiming to be none other than Inez herself. Then came the sounds of child-like footsteps running up and down the length of the second-floor hallway, and what sounded like a young girl giggling.

I suppose it's possible that the ghost of Inez somehow spontaneously decided to turn up at Malvern Manor more than a century after her death, which just coincidentally happened to take place when she was being talked about on a regular basis there. But I find the more compelling argument to be that all of the storytelling either created a thought form, which then began to sound and behave like a little girl, or an opportunistic entity assumed the identity of Inez and started pretending to be her, perhaps for its own amusement.

It is not a demon, and it is not the spirit of the killer, the article goes on. I find these both to be very credible statements.

For his part, Chris Dedman *does* ascribe a demonic influence to the haunting of the Villisca Axe Murder House. Once again, we're keeping an open mind in that regard. Others have reported encountering something inside the property that they believed to have been non-human in nature, and this may be an avenue worthy of further investigation.

What intrigues Sarah and I is Dawn's contention that the

negative thought-form was not an after-effect of the Villisca Axe Murders — she believes that the entity was actually there first.

Dawn goes on to point out that thousands, if not tens of thousands of people have visited the former Moore residence since the murders, many of them seeking a brush with the macabre and to make some connection with the grisly events of June 9/10, 1912. That's a lot of negative energy, which could potentially have acted as a food source for such a thought form, nourishing it and encouraging it to remain at the house in the same way that a dog rarely strays too far from its food dish.

This intriguing possibility sets my mind racing, and I just have to talk to Dawn in person. Fortunately, she's gracious enough to consent to a phone conversation. As somebody who claims to have sensitive abilities, I was particularly interested in her impressions of what haunts the Villisca Axe Murder House.

"What we were interacting with was in the ground floor bedroom," Dawn begins, after we've exchanged greetings. "At first, it seemed to be a small child...but as time went on, there were small bursts of a very different vibe. When these bursts came through, they were *extremely* noticeable."

Dawn adds that having done this for quite a few years, she isn't easily fooled when a heavier, more dominant entity tries to pass itself off a something much lighter and childlike.

She's convinced that this being was trying to manipulate her into thinking it was something that it really wasn't — sweet and innocent.

We discuss the opinion advanced by Amy Allan on *The Dead Files,* that the spirit haunting the Stillinger girls' bedroom is indeed that of a little girl — one who likes to growl at people like Johnny Houser in order to give them a good scare. Dawn does not agree.

"The growls are coming from this entity's natural state," she explains. "It's a form of communication used by this thing that is there, this thing that has people believing that it's Lena."

Dawn tells me that she perceived a very dark entity manifesting up in the attic. She describes it as "a shadow mass," although it did not assume the snake-like form reported by at least one other visitor to the house.

"This thing would *pulse*, almost," she goes on, "and as it pulsed, it would push out through the surrounding walls."

Our topic of conversation turns toward something that I'd read in her blog post that intrigued me: Dawn's belief that whatever it was that haunts the Villisca Axe Murder House actually predates the murders.

"Thought forms basically *record* experiences. It's had so many experiences in that house over all this time, soaking up the emotions and the intent behind them like a sponge." Dawn thinks it's possible that this particular entity may have already been in the area in 1912, and might have exerted some influence over the murders taking place. "Think of this negative thought form somehow mixing with another source of strong negative energy, and those murders are the result."

I'm reminded of Reverend George Kelly's claim in his confession that he was compelled to kill by a voice and overcome by some kind of higher influence. Although some believe it to be true (or key parts of it, at least) many scholars of the Villisca Axe Murders dismiss Kelly's confession as being nothing more that the ramblings of a madman...just not those of a *homicidal* madman. Could it be possible that there is some truth to his claims after all?

"It would have to have been a person who was already extremely negative," she continues, "in order to provoke them into doing something so savage. I think the murderer was a person who was already heading in that direction."

I ask Dawn who she thinks that person might have been. "The drifter," she replies, without hesitation. "I don't think this crime was a one-off, and there are reports of similar killings along the railroad that were probably done by the same person."

I tend to agree with her.

Going back to the matter of the entity which she believes haunts the house, I ask Dawn whether it has a specific goal in mind, other than to feed on negative energy.

"The feeding is just a byproduct of what it does. Its

purpose is essentially to create chaos, because that's just its nature. This is a multi-faceted type of energy, something which we [the many visitors to the house] have helped to create."

"Is it intelligent?" I ask, curious. "It does seem to enjoying playing roles."

"Yes, it does," she agrees. "And there were moments during our investigation when it would seem to pull back from us, seeming to leave the house completely. That's when the barn started to feel off."

I can't help but be reminded of the comments made by Stephen and Amy Allan about the killer's energy being strongest in the barn. Could this be what Dawn had been picking up on too? I'm starting to regret not having spent more time investigating the barn, but then she goes on to tell me that she slept in the barn overnight, and experienced nothing other than the feeling of coldness that comes with sleeping in an unheated wooden structure.

By the time we hang up, my conversation with Dawn has left me with more food for thought. Her experiences at Villisca dovetail with Johnny Houser's theory about the house itself being behind it all — the house, that is, as personified by the negative entity in question. Perhaps the two are one and the same, the entity and the structure long since fused into an inseparable hybrid.

There's only one thing I can say for sure: I need to dig a

little deeper into this particular mystery, and that means going back.

CHAPTER ELEVEN
A Glimpse of Hell

I recently found myself on a panel at a pop culture convention with film-maker Seth Alne and his brother, Jesse. The theme of the panel was "Haunted Iowa," and while I was speaking about my book on Malvern Manor, the Alne brothers were relating their experiences at Villisca. Once I heard what they had gone through, I knew that I had to learn more about it, and arranged for an interview with Seth.

He and Jesse first visited the Villisca Axe Murder House in 2007. They were relatively new to the world of paranormal investigation at the time, and when the opportunity arose for them to spend the night there, they jumped at the chance. Putting together a group of five, they were excited to set foot in one of Iowa's most infamous haunted houses.

Standing in the parlor, they were surprised to hear the sound of voices coming from up above them. The second floor was supposed to be empty...as, indeed, it proved to be when they checked.

Later, while he was sitting there quietly and just taking in the atmosphere, Seth was amazed to see that the EMF meter that he had next to him on the arm of the chair was now spinning in slow circles. He watched it spin lazily for a moment, and then said "Stop that." It stopped dead, as though influenced by an unseen force. He's adamant that the meter didn't slow down at all — it went from a fast spin to a complete stop in just a split-second.

He was still processing this strange turn of events when he felt something tugging at the hem of his shorts. From behind his head, the sound of a little girl's voice singing began coming through the wall. In his own words, "I just freaking lost it."

His hands started shaking. When he played back the audio recording later, the soft, melodious tune had not been picked up, but Seth is adamant about what he heard.

Seth had no further doubt as to whether the Villisca Axe Murder House might be haunted. He *knew* it was.

"The thing that always strikes me about Villisca is how it *feels*," Seth recalls. "When you walk into that house, you just know...you *feel* what happened there. You never feel comfortable or at ease there."

What is it that Seth believes haunts the former Moore residence? "I call it the soul of the house. It is pretty much a sponge, and it has sucked up all of the evil that has happened there. I don't think there are multiple entities there. There's just this *one* thing, and it acts all of the parts..."

That's an intriguing premise, and one I'd never really thought of in that way before.

"Jesse and two other investigators saw this big, black, shadowy mass inside that house. It had two huge red eyes.

The thing appeared in the attic doorway, and all three of them just *froze.* They couldn't talk or move a muscle. One of them began bawling their eyes out. Jesse said that it slithered up to him—"

"Slithered?" I interject. That's a very interesting choice of word, conjuring up images of something reptilian, snake-like.

"Slithered," Seth confirms. "It was all Jesse could do to cover his face with his hands. The thing started hissing at him. This is the evil entity that we think is the soul of the house. I think it has been there ever since the house was made, and that *it* is what pushed the killer to do what he did."

If I understand him correctly, Seth is proposing that the murders weren't premeditated, but rather, that an intruder was driven to murder, influenced by an evil outside force. He believes that the only explanation for one man killing so many victims without any of them getting out of bed to fight back, was that this man had help — and not of the human kind.

He points to the confession made by Reverend George Kelly, who claimed that God told him to do it — "to slay, and slay utterly." This voice, Seth infers, was not the voice of God at all, but rather, the malign influence which lies behind the haunting of the Villisca Axe Murder House.

Seth's brother, Jesse, speaks of having had his own

encounter with this entity, and it left him with no desire to ever investigate a haunted location again. Jesse was down in the basement of the house, an area that my team and I had done little more than visit for half an hour to run burst EVP sessions — and found nothing.

Jesse watched as a vortex of black smoke drifted out of the cellar wall. A dark, snake-like creature emerged from within the smoke, and slowly began to coil itself around his legs. "He's seeing this in his mind's eye," explains Seth, "but to him, it's completely real. The others in the basement with him didn't experience it at all."

The snake kept slithering up his body, rearing up in front of Jesse. When it reached eye level, its head turned into a female face. He got up and ran out of the cellar, fleeing to the barn. When Seth found him, Jesse had his head in his hands, and kept repeating the phrase *"All I see is Hell,"* over and over again.

According to Seth, for the next hour, his brother kept seeing flashes of the Biblical Hell, with souls being cast into lakes of fire or being torn apart.

"He was *white*, man. Just pure, unadulterated fear on his face. I took him off the property, out into the street, and started praying over him. That's when it started to, kind of, *lift*. But even right now, he can close his eyes and still see what he saw that day."

Seth has no doubt that his brother came close to being

possessed that day. He believes that the haunting is demonic in nature, and is not afraid to say so. "Enough people have gotten legitimate scratches at Villisca, yeah...it all comes back to an interaction with a demon. Whatever this thing is, it wants to cause fear. Anything could happen in that house...including murder.

"It's hard to believe some of the interactions I've had and seen in the Axe Murder House. Three times, over a Ghost Box, the sound of a killer confessing. In one session, there was a full explanation that Frank Jones paid a guy to do this. This thing at Villisca, it likes to put on a show. It'll tell you whatever it is you want to hear. It messes with people."

As our interview wraps up, he gives me one last piece of advice. "That house...you gotta know what you're doing, if you're going to go to that house. It's not something to joke around with."

The next time I talk to Johnny Houser, he corroborates the story about Jesse's experience. Then, after thinking for a moment, he adds, "Seth and Jesse are two of the most honorable people who have ever investigated here at Villisca."

Johnny's word is good enough for me. I resolve to be extra careful the next time I step over the threshold of the Villisca Axe Murder House.

CHAPTER TWELVE
Houser Cards

There's no way you can learn enough about the Villisca Axe Murder House over the space of just one or two nights there, and so I always knew that I'd need to make multiple visits to the property if I was to stand any chance of understanding the haunting.

My companions for this trip are two highly seasoned paranormal investigators and personal friends. We've worked together numerous times before, and I trust their skills and integrity implicitly.

Stephen is a professional musician, specializing in the cello. He gives music lessons out of a beautiful mountain studio. When he isn't doing that, Stephen travels around the country, visiting haunted locations and researching them. As a priest representing the Old Catholic Church, he has the theological aspects covered in addition to the more prosaic ones. This is the same Stephen who advised Sarah and I on where best to concentrate our investigative efforts. He was calling in on the phone then; now he's accompanying me in person.

Erik makes a living in the field of I.T. He's also an accomplished author of paranormal non-fiction, writing about his experiences at some of the same haunted places that he has investigated. One of those locations is the Farrar

School in Iowa, not too far from Villisca. In fact, he and I are planning on co-authoring a book about our investigation of the school. (It will subsequently come to be published under the title *A Haunting at Farrar*).

As road trips go, it's a fun one. Our first overnight stop is at Malvern Manor, which just so happens to be on our way. After spending the night at Malvern, we spend three more days carrying out research at Farrar. The old school is mysterious and full of character. It's also paranormally active, and all three of us agree that our long road trip has already been proven to be well worthwhile.

And now comes Villisca.

It's early in the afternoon when we hit town after a relatively short drive from Farrar. Although we're on the tired side after spending the last few nights staying awake, we're excited to see what the next sixteen hours will bring. Erik drives, and can't help but doze a little as the cornfields and farmland roll by. Iowa has proven to be a beautiful place, with beautiful scenery and friendly people. We've been made to feel very welcome.

Erik and Stephen have both been to Villisca before. A little before four o'clock, we pull into a parking space outside the Moore house. There have been several tours of people throughout the day, and the last, a party of four — two men and two women, all in their twenties — is leaving. Rather than the somber looks one would expect to see on the faces of visitors to the scene of a mass murder, they're laughing and joking as they exit the house and walk back to their vehicle. Their obvious lack of respect leaves a sour taste in my mouth.

Stephen and Erik head inside to sign the paperwork that will grant us access for the night, and emerge a few minutes later with the key, which is chained to the handle of a hatchet in order to prevent it being lost. Erik leads us up the wooden ramp to the covered porch. Unlocking the door and swinging it open, he's the first to step into the house. As I follow him through, I can't help but wonder (not for the first time) whether this is the same door through which the killer made entry on the night of the murders. It's a sobering thought.

We take baseline EMF readings throughout the property and quite understandably find nothing. It would be strange if we did. After all, the electrical wiring was all stripped out of the house during the restoration process. Now, the only remaining concession to the twenty-first century is a single extension cable, which runs in through the window of the Stillinger girls' bedroom on the ground floor.

The kitchen door opens with a theatrical creak. We all look up.

"Hello?" a familiar voice says. Johnny Houser walks

into the house. He's lost a bit of weight and muscled up since his last TV appearance. This new healthy lifestyle and fitness regime really suits him. Even his muscles have muscles. He's effusive and friendly, shaking hands all round and exchanging pleasantries before finally taking a seat in the corner of the parlor.

Johnny Houser is one of those people you just instinctively warm to right away. He has been inside the house for no more than thirty seconds before there is a huge double thud-boom, the sound of something very expensive and very heavy hitting the ground somewhere else in the house...or so we think.

"What was that?" I ask, always Captain Obvious. "That was loud!"

"Good question," says Stephen.

We split up and search the house from top to bottom. Nothing is out of place. None of the furniture has fallen over. Chairs and dressers are still standing upright, just as they were on our initial walk-through a few minutes before. We can't find a single thing to explain it. Yet the impact, whatever it was, was violent enough to shake the entire house.

I can't help but suspect that Johnny has just acted as some kind of catalyst. The timing is too fortuitous.

"I thought for sure some shit fell down somewhere," Erik says, shaking his head. We're all puzzled.

"It was loud alright," Johnny agrees. He can offer nothing in the way of an explanation. Stephen and Erik were running a Tascam high-quality audio recorder at the top of the stairs, and my own digital voice recorder was set up to record our conversation with Johnny. When we check, both devices pick up the boom.

Conversation turns to Stephen and Erik's previous experiences investigating the house, three years prior, with their team, the American Association of Paranormal Investigators (AAPI). Erik and Stephen play some of their findings for Johnny.

They had gone out for dinner, locking the house up and leaving three audio recorders running, all in different parts of the house. Only one of them picked up anything strange, but that something was an absolute doozy: the sound of a child talking to itself. It's an absolutely incredible find. Jill, Stephen, and Erik are all grown adults. Their voices do not sound the least bit child-like. There is no way that the voice on the recording could possibly have belonged to one of them; even if they had tried to imitate a child's vocal characteristics and speech pattern, even a casual listener would be able to tell the difference.

In my opinion, what they inadvertently recorded was one hundred percent paranormal in nature. Even Johnny seems impressed with it. I know that I most certainly am. Could the voice belong to one of the murdered children? It's a disturbing thought, but even more chilling is the possibility that it may instead come from something entirely different...something that is imitating them to suit its own purposes.

Erik cues up the next audio file. What's fascinating about this particular EVP is that the three investigators from AAPI were all sequestered in the kitchen at the time. One of them was regaling the others with a funny anecdote, which earned her a chuckle from them both. At the same time, a digital voice recorder, which had been left running in the master bedroom at the top of the staircase, picked up the disembodied laugh — a laugh that, based upon its volume compared to the voices of the three paranormal investigators, is much closer to the microphone than they are. It's almost as if they are being eavesdropped on from the top of the stairs, in the same way that children will sometimes eavesdrop on their parents downstairs when they are supposed to be tucked up in bed and fast asleep.

Another crystal-clear, Class A EVP can be heard saying the name *Joseph.* At first, I wondered if the name could have been *Josiah,* but that would have been a little too neat and easy. The voice sounds feminine, to my ear, though it is by no means one hundred percent certain. It was recorded in the Moore childrens' bedroom up on the second floor, as was another EVP, recorded shortly after. This one is much more difficult to make out, although it plainly is not something spoken by any of the investigators who are present.

Johnny sits forward, hands interlaced in his lap, eyes closed, listening intently. At the time of the AAPI investigation, Villisca was being rocked by a thunderstorm which would have been considered violent in many places, but only moderate by the standards of Iowa. (Iowans are a very hardy bunch of people). Thunder can be heard rolling and booming in the background of each recording, like a creeping artillery barrage that stands in stark contrast to the pleasant, sunny weather that we have outside right now. If this was a horror movie, then it would have the perfect "dark and stormy night" soundtrack going on.

In another EVP, a softly-whispering voice, its gender impossible to make out, echoes an Ovilus device by repeating the word *coat* a few seconds afterward. This wasn't the only whisper caught by the AAPI team. No sooner had they taken custody of the house for the night, before they had even fully unpacked all of their equipment, their recorders captured the sound of a female voice saying the words *"I'm coming in..."* It's absolutely a Class A capture.

A more disturbing EVP appears to be hissing the words *"That bastard!"* Again, it's difficult to determine the gender of the speaker, let alone their identity, but Erik and Stephen are adamant that it is absolutely not one of the AAPI crew. Knowing them all personally and being familiar with their voices, I completely agree.

(I encourage you to listen to the EVPs they gathered by visiting *www.ghostpi.com/villisca* and judge them for yourself).

Once the EVPs are done, I ask Johnny a few questions about the haunting and his experiences with the house. He is, after all, "Mister Villisca," the acknowledged expert on paranormal activity at this particular location. I can't wait to get his unique perspective on it all.

Johnny first came to the Villisca Axe Murder House some fifteen years ago. He wasn't remotely prepared for the things he would ultimately encounter, both within its walls and then finally within the walls of his own home.

Darwin, the owner of the house, had told him with a smile that "the kids will hug you, maybe kiss you on the hand sometimes." Johnny had started out trying to connect with the spirits of the children by bringing them a ball and trying to get them to roll it back to him. They never did. After putting some thought into it, Johnny asked himself why he would ever have thought that a bunch of kids would be anything other than scared of a big, bearded stranger like him.

One day, something about the unfairness of it all managed to get to him. The idea that six innocent, helpless children had been murdered here made him so angry. He stomped into the attic and had to vent, having a bit of a rant to clear the air. *"SIX KIDS!"* he growled through gritted teeth, both fists clenched angrily at his sides.

The sounds of footsteps in the hallway outside stopped him dead in his tracks. He was running a voice recorder at the time, and not only did it pick up the sound of the footsteps, it also caught the rumble of a low, menacing growl. Something apparently didn't like being provoked.

At that particular time, the house was getting a lot of visitors who would adopt a belligerent attitude, coming in and commanding the ghosts to name themselves and the killer. Johnny finds that laughable. "Like they're going to obey your commands," he says, shaking his head. "There's so much going on here that has *nothing* to do with the axe murders. I think there's an element of the house haunting itself, and I think that we're partly responsible."

"We?" I ask, frowning.

"Everybody that comes here and does the paranormal circuit. Malvern. Farrar. Edinburgh Manor. Then on to Villisca. Who knows exactly what energies and spirits came here from, say, Farrar, or Malvern Manor?"

In other words, people like *us*.

He's absolutely right about that, I realize. We've just come from Farrar ourselves. Who's to say that we haven't brought a phantom school kid along with us, without knowing it? We did engage in psychic protection before we left, but there are never any one hundred percent guarantees.

"I hope and pray that the murdered kids are not here," he goes on. "I hope they've moved on, that they're in Heaven, and that they're having the time of their lives."

We wholeheartedly agree with him. There are few thoughts more disturbing than the idea that more than a century after their deaths, those poor children could still be stuck within the same four walls, perhaps reliving that awful night over and over again.

Johnny goes on to tell us about another strange period in the history of the house. It had been an event run by TAPS, the group featured in the TV show *Ghost Hunters*. Johnny had mentioned to them that a number of EVPs had recently come through that were spoken in the French language. After the event had concluded, two of the organizers came through to the office in the barn where he had been hanging out and said, "Dude, we asked questions in French, and we got EVP replies in French..."

"This house is just weird," he continues. "One night, the group will tell us that they had a perfectly pleasant, uneventful evening. The next night, they'll flee because something happens that makes them feel unsafe. You can never tell which it's going to be."

The three of us look sideways at one another. We all know which one *we'd* like it to be, given the choice.

"So how are your investigations going here now?" I ask. Johnny shakes his head.

"I won't investigate this place ever again."

Now, *that* comes as a surprise. "You won't?" I ask. "Why?"

Johnny sighs, leaning back into the chair as though he's settling in to tell us a long and difficult story. It had all begun with a series he'd filmed for the VidiSpace platform, titled *Johnny Houser versus the Villisca Axe Murder House*.

"Whenever I investigate here, stuff starts happening at my house," he says. That tracks with what he'd told Steve DiSchiavi and Amy Allan during the *Dead Files* episode. He'd been very open about the fact that paranormal activity often crosses over from the Moore House to his own. At the time, I thought of it as being simply a cost of doing business, as it were, an unavoidable side effect of taking work home with you even though you don't want to.

One night, Johnny had a very strange and disturbing dream, in which he was in the basement of his home and an intruder broke in. The intruder was carrying a camera.

"What are you doing?" Dream-Johnny demanded.

"Oh, we've got permission to film here," came the reply.

"Did Darwin give you permission?" Dream-Johnny asked, knowing full well that Darwin Linn had already been dead for several years.

"Yeah, we talked to him yesterday..." the intruder said. Even though he was dreaming, Johnny knew that this just wasn't right. Suddenly, he could hear his wife screaming from elsewhere in the house.

That's when he woke up.

A worrisome thought began to nag at him. *That's exactly what I'm doing over there, to them. Busting into their house, waving a camera around...*It made him wonder about the effects his paranormal research might be having on the spirit inhabitants of the Moore House.

It was morning, and time for him to make the school run with his young daughter. The drive was a short one, and Johnny arrived home a few minutes later. His wife told him that she had just had a disturbing dream of her own: or more accurately, a nightmare, in which Sara Moore was hitting her repeatedly in the face, wanting to inflict similar injuries to those that she had sustained in the Axeman's savage attack.

That's when a light bulb went off over his head, figuratively speaking. Everything suddenly became clear. Throwing on a coat, Johnny went straight over to the Moore House, which was currently standing empty, the previous night's investigators having already left.

Letting himself in, he walked into the parlor and spoke into thin air, addressing the spirits of the house.

"I get it," he said. "I'm done. I have four episodes of my show left to film, and then I'm done investigating here for good."

He paused. If Johnny was expecting a response, none was forthcoming. The house was totally silent. Yet who knows how many sets of eyes were watching and listening to him from the shadows?

"And... I'm *sorry*. You guys get this every night, and you don't need it coming from me on top of all that. I'm so sorry."

True to his word, although he stills books in visitors and maintains the place, he has never conducted another paranormal investigation inside the Villisca Axe Murder House since then.

"I get it," I finally tell him. And I really do. A man surely has to draw a line in the sand when it comes to the welfare of his own family.

"Don't get me wrong, it really kind of sucks," Johnny chuckles. "I have the keys 24/7, and this place is literally on my doorstep. A paranormal investigator's dream, right here for the taking. But the right thing to do is the right thing to do."

Next up, we change the subject a little. I want to pick Johnny's brain as to his opinion on the possible identity of the killer...or killers.

"So, Reverend Kelly, the weird minister who confessed—"Johnny begins.

"*Weird minister,* Stephen," I laugh, pointing at my

friend. "Weird *priest!*"

"Oh God," Stephen rolls his eyes in a manner which suggests that he's imploring the good Lord, his boss, for strength.

"—a voice told him to rise up and slay, and a shadow was in the back yard here that he claimed gave him the axe. He said that he walked in this door at 1 a.m." — Johnny gestures behind him toward the closed door — "and killed the kids upstairs first, then killed the parents, and finally killed the Stillinger girls last. Kelly said that he didn't even know that they were in there; he only found them because he wanted to take a nap afterwards."

That doesn't make a lot of sense to me, in terms of motive. For one thing, a number of experts on both the Villisca case and violent crime in general have agreed that there was a significant sexual component to the crime, in the form of Lena Stillinger's post-mortem treatment. If Reverend Kelly really did not know that the two Stillinger sisters were present in the house, was his defilement of Lena's body nothing more than a crime of opportunity, rather than being premeditated?

"Anyway, despite him being a Peeping Tom, he was acquitted," Johnny goes on. "He made some outrageous claims, saying that he worked for the Queen of England. His story just doesn't add up. The general consensus is that whoever did this, was hiding up there in the attic." Johnny looks upward toward the ceiling. "But we'll never really know for sure."

"We won't," I agree, "but if you had to put your money on one of the suspects, which one would it be?"

"The Man from the Train," Johnny replies. "I believe that theory. A few weeks ago, fifteen Supreme Court judges came down here to visit, just for the educational experience of it all. They all thought the same thing. You can trace the pattern of murders so easily...starting around 1902, it goes all the way across the Midwest, to the East Coast, the West Coast..." Now he starts checking off the points on his fingers, one by one. "They're always following the train tracks. The axe used as a murder weapon was always found on the property. The houses were all locked, the families always in bed. Mirrors were always covered...it's the same thing, over and over again."

He's absolutely correct. The James' outline much of this in their book on the case, as does Troy Taylor in his own study of the Midwest Axe Murders. Once you know where to look for them, the similarities between each set of murders are stark and glaring.

Johnny also points out that as the string of murders progressed, the crime scenes that the killer left behind him became cleaner and less chaotic. "It's likely that he was getting better at what he did with each successful murder, that he was getting a little slicker each time out."

He raises an interesting point. Most serial killers, after they have gained an initial amount of experience from their first few successful murders, then become complacent. They grow sloppy, becoming used to getting away with their crimes. That sloppiness is what usually gets them caught. Yet this did not happen in the case of the Villisca Axe Man, so far as we are aware.

"I don't buy into it being a hired hit, or anybody local," Johnny says, dismissing those theories with a wave of his hand. "It wasn't Frank Jones, the politician. I read twenty years' worth of his personal letters and documents. He just wasn't the kind of guy that would do something like this. Especially not to children. I saw his personal Bible. It had highlighted passages of *Love Thy Neighbor*."

Stephen, Erik and I all nod in agreement. "I can understand somebody killing adults to serve some goal," I say, "but it takes a special kind of twisted monster to kill children.

"Who could live with doing something like that?" Johnny asks rhetorically. "That's one of the things that keeps me in this place. I was ready to move on at one point. This job was supposed to be a temporary thing. Always said to myself, *Johnny, You're an investigator, not a tour guide.*

"Back in the early days, I treated it as a lab. When I acknowledged that it really was haunted, I started to look for patterns. I wanted to know if the paranormal activity tracked with storms, the days of the week, phases of the Moon..."

That reference to the days of the week jogs my memory, reminding me of something I've always wanted to know. "Johnny, is the house any more active on the anniversary of the murders than it is on any other night of the year?"

He pauses for a moment to consider his answer. "I've investigated here on six or seven of those nights. All of them were pretty active, except for the hundred-year anniversary in 2012. Nothing happened that night, weirdly enough. Not a thing. But every June 9, there's so much anxiety in this house, it becomes overwhelming. It just builds, builds, builds, builds...and then, at a certain time of the night..." Johnny makes a chopping motion with one hand. "Done. On June 10, it's just eerily calm. There's a feeling of *it's over*, all through the house. Then the cycle starts all over again the next year."

The phenomenon of anniversary hauntings is a well-established one in the literature of paranormal research, but it's one that I've always found to be rather curious. A year is, of course, the period of time that it takes for the Earth to move around the Sun. What is it, paranormally speaking, that would make phenomena intensify every 365 days like clockwork, before somehow dissipating, only to start up all over again and building toward the same thing 365 days later? Why not every two years? Or five? Or fifty? Do ghosts read calendars and keep track of the passage of time (I ask this question largely in a tongue-in-cheek sort of way) or is this purely a psychological phenomenon, one which says more about the way in which the human mind works than it does about the objective nature of a haunting?

One day, Johnny was working upstairs in the Axe Murder House, fixing one of the beds in the Moore children's room. He had made a point of locking the door behind him when he entered, to keep out any uninvited visitors of the flesh and blood variety. Johnny was down on his knees, tightening up a bolt on the bed frame, when he suddenly heard a loud *thud*, followed by the sound of something being dragged across the floor downstairs. It was accompanied by the sound of very distinct footsteps.

As he listened, breathing quietly and straining his ears, Johnny could hear the footsteps travel across the kitchen floor to the foot of the staircase. Then they began to climb, taking each step one at a time, echoing with a dull, percussive *thud, thud, thud* that came slowly, inexorably toward him through the master bedroom.

It was past nightfall, and Johnny was working by the light of a Coleman electric lantern. Inside the house, everything beyond the small circle of light that it gave off was pitch blackness. For reasons that he still cannot put into words, Johnny went into the closet and pulled the door shut behind him.

That's stupid, he thought to himself. *Now I'm just stuck in the closet.* As plans went, he realized that this one wasn't particularly well thought-out.

Through the firmly-closed door, he could hear the muffled sound of the footsteps coming into the children's bedroom. They were loud and heavy, the sort of footsteps that a man wearing boots would make on bare wooden flooring. From where he stood, hunched over inside the closet, Johnny could just make out the dull white glow of the lantern light in the gap underneath the door. As he watched, something solid passed between the light and the door, blotting it out for a split-second.

At this point in time, the thought of ghosts was far from his mind. He considered it much more likely that an intruder had broken into the house, unaware that its caretaker was fixing a bed up on the second floor. It would take an exceptionally brave — or stupid, take your pick — burglar to break into the Villisca Axe Murder House, but that's exactly what Johnny suspected was going on.

What the intruder didn't know was that Johnny was armed.

"Alright," he called out. "I've got a loaded 9mm pistol with me, and I'm coming out in three seconds."

He wasn't bluffing. Johnny reached down to his hip and wrapped his fingers around the grip. It was reassuringly solid.

"One."

The weapon cleared its holster. Johnny brought it up in front of him.

"Two."

He disengaged the safety catch. From the other side of the door, there came not a sound.

"Three."

He reached out and pushed the closet door open, then brought his hand back onto the grip to steady the pistol as it came up into the ready position. Johnny was a competent marksman, and at such close range, it would be like shooting fish in a barrel.

Except nobody was there.

The bedroom was completely empty, save for the shadows cast on the walls by the lantern light, which turned the wrought-iron bed frames into something that looked more like twisted monsters. But of the noisy intruder, there was absolutely no sign.

Johnny cleared the rest of the house, moving slowly and methodically from room to room. Duck-walking through the low attic doorway induced a little anxiety, but it turned out to be every bit as empty as the rest of the house.

"Son of a bitch," was all he could think of to say. The doors were still locked, the windows closed, and there were no signs of breaking and entering. He was the only living soul in the Villisca Axe Murder House...with a pulse, at least.

Later, after his heart rate dropped back down to something close to its normal level, Johnny had a chance to give the encounter some thought. Now, with the benefit of hindsight, he's convinced that what he experienced that night was a completely residual phenomenon, a paranormal after-echo of the events that happened on the night of the murders. Whatever the source of the footsteps was, it was no more capable of interacting with Johnny than the images on his TV screen would have been. It had, however, given him the fright of his life.

It's been a real privilege to sit and interview Johnny, but his time with us is now coming to a close. We all stand up, the sound of four middle-aged men getting to their feet scarily close to the soundtrack from a late-night movie, and shake hands.

"Any last-minute advice as to how best to approach this place?" I ask him as he makes his way into the kitchen. "Tech? No tech? A mix?"

Johnny puffs out his cheeks, thinking. "Just do your thing," he says at last. "This house is going to do whatever it wants to do, no matter which approach you guys take. So just treat it with respect and try to enjoy yourselves. At the end of the day, you're going to get what you're going to get."

"Thanks Johnny."

We walk him to the kitchen door. He stops and turns around, suddenly remembering something.

"The one thing I really don't like about this place is the whole mental mindfuck aspect of it," he says. "It's got some kind of *Amityville Horror* aspects to it. If you read the visitor guest books, accounts that were written by people who came here for the night, a lot of them talk about the house somehow pitting them against each other. Making them mad, getting friends to turn on one another. Just watch yourselves, okay?"

And on that note, he's gone.

CHAPTER THIRTEEN
"For Fun."

Johnny's certainly right about one thing: the guest books *do* make for fascinating reading. A surprising number of visitors have felt compelled to record their experiences for posterity, and I spend a couple of hours sitting in the barn, leafing through them all and looking for commonalities.

A lot of them report being overwhelmed by sudden feelings of emotional upset. That makes complete sense, when one considers the blanket of sadness that constantly permeates the house. But I find several instances of people who were fine one minute, and then reduced to tears the next, all of them taken completely by surprise. It makes me wonder whether there's something in the house which is making these people experience such emotions a great deal more acutely than they otherwise would. I resolve to watch my own mood, and those of my companions, very closely over the course of our investigation.

Also very common are reports of visitors being touched by unseen hands, or feeling sudden temperature variations — usually going ice-cold all over, when everybody else around them felt just fine. Several made a point of noting that the air conditioning was switched off at the time. Nausea, headaches, and various aches and pains also deserve an honorary mention here; it's impossible to say how many of these might be genuinely paranormal, and how many are simply psychosomatic in nature.

A rare few claimed to have sustained actual physical injuries. One such incident involved a male visitor developing a spontaneous burn on his leg. Another reported being scratched in the shape of a letter V.

Spirit boxes tend to be very chatty inside the Villisca Axe Murder House, and digital voice recorders often yield an unusually high number of EVPs. I found multiple reports of the names *Sara, Boyd*, and *Paul* coming through on such devices. Cries for help are also very common, which is unsurprising, given the history of the house. The idea that some of the victims may still be present after so many years is a distressing one. Next to the frequent calls for help, *get out!* is also extremely common.

Ouija boards are also prone to spelling out the names of the dead victims, particularly that of Lena. Phantom footsteps were also recorded by several people, and seem to fall into two categories: either the playful and child-like, or heavy and menacing.

All in all, there are over a hundred documented encounters in the visitor logs of the Villisca Axe Murder House, with more being added each week. I close the folder, lock up the barn, and head back to the house. There's a very light breeze rustling the leaves and grass as I climb the wooden ramp.

Stephen and Erik have been hard at work, running EVP burst sessions and placing trigger objects at strategic points around the house. They ask if I want to join them in the parlor for the next one, and I'm happy to participate.

"You lead off," Erik says, presumably sick of talking to the dead and getting no answers so far.

"Why's it so quiet?" I ask, looking around the dimly-lit parlor. Stephen had a glowing red flashlight sitting in one of the wall-mounted sconces, the main source of light in the room. When I ask my next question — "Who made the bang when Johnny came in?" — the flashlight immediately switches itself off. The room is plunged into darkness.

"What?" Stephen grunts, bemused.

"Can you turn the flashlight back on, please?" I ask. Five seconds pass. Then it switches itself back on. *"SHIT!"* I exclaim, impressed.

There's a so-called investigative method — I use the term loosely — employed by paranormal investigators, known as the flashlight trick. At one point, I even used it myself, though I soon learned why it was a poor idea. The flashlight trick involves taking a MagLite, and unscrewing the head from the body a little. After the MagLite has been running for a few minutes, it will usually start to dim, brighten, then switch itself off and on. Contrary to popular belief, this has nothing to do with ghosts, and everything to do with the fact that the metal inside the MagLite expands and contracts relative to temperature variations. When the bulb is powered on, the light gets hotter; when it's off, it gets cooler. This cycle of swelling and shrinking causes the electrical contacts to come together and then separate on an intermittent basis, causing the unwary to think that the MagLite is being manipulated by spirits.

The reason I went into detail explaining the flashlight trick is that I wanted to be clear about one thing: it *only* works on the screw-head MagLite type of flashlight. Stephen's flashlight, on the other hand, uses an LED. It doesn't have the same type of electrical contacts that a MagLite would. Which makes it even more strange that it would switch itself off on command.

Using another pocket light with which to see, Stephen gently lifts the LED flashlight down from its sconce and examines it carefully. The power switch is in the *on* position. This wasn't some inexplicable power drain or brownout. The only way in which his light could possibly have gone out is for the switch to have been manually slid into place. In other words, something has just physically shut down his flashlight and then switched it back on again when I asked it to.

To say that I'm impressed would be putting it mildly. I can't stop myself from laughing with delight. Stephen joins in. Erik, as per usual, looks pensive.

"Thank you, if that was you!" I say, meaning every word

of it.

I see Erik turn his head toward the head, as though reacting to something. He is. As a sensitive who has been working on fine-tuning his abilities, he sometimes picks up on certain kinds of energies when we're at haunted locations.

"I don't know how to put it into words, but it was on the stairs, and now it's in here," he tells us. "It's more a kind of...feeling of spacial displacement. And now it's gone."

Stephen, who has better-developed psychic sensibilities, says that he feels it go straight through him. I'm standing there watching the two of them, feeling about as useful as a chocolate tea pot. It's always like this when sensitives start comparing notes. I'm not remotely sensitive, so the best I can do is hang back and observe. Always a bridesmaid, never a bride, as the old saying goes.

We try another burst EVP session. This time, Stephen leads. He has a calm and soothing voice, making him ideally suited for this kind of experiment. Erik and I stay quiet and let him work, each of us running a digital voice recorder of our own.

It runs for two minutes. Then we play back the audio recording from Stephen's device. No sooner has he cued it up than we hear a thud coming from behind him, somewhere in the Stillinger girls' bedroom. I shine my flashlight in there. Nothing is out of place, and the air conditioning is off.

After checking the recording out thoroughly, we concede

that there are no EVPs this time. Disappointing, perhaps, but the LED flashlight activity more than makes up for it. And there's more to come.

Stephen's LED light begins strobing, pulsing itself off and on in a rapid sequence. There's a special setting which allows it to do this, but it requires that the operator activate it manually by pushing a button in a certain way. Nobody has touched it, however; the flashlight has spent the last few minutes sitting back up there in its sconce.

"Has it ever acted like this before?" I ask. Stephen shakes his head in the negative. It's very peculiar behavior for a piece of technology like this, almost as if there's an unseen somebody fooling around with the flashlight right in front of our eyes.

Another thud from the Stillinger sisters' room. There's nothing in there, other than the AC unit, with any moving parts — and it's been shut down for hours. In the distance, the sound of a train sounding its horn drifts across on the still night air. Every time I hear this at Villisca, and it happens *a lot,* it sends a chill down my spine, perhaps because it's an audible reminder of the Man from the Train and the pure evil that he represents.

The LED flashlight begins to pulse again. Stephen takes it down and examines it. Slides the power switch back and forth a few times. "It's completely dead."

"When did you last charge it?" Erik asks.

"It was fully charged when we came in. It didn't even make it an hour."

With freshly-charged batteries in place, the priest puts the flashlight back in the sconce. It behaves itself for the next hour, while we do a series of EVP sessions, and just as we're starting to conclude that it was some kind of funky electrical issue related to those particular batteries, the flashlight starts switching itself off and on again.

"It's not the batteries," says Erik. Stephen will go on to use the same LED flashlight for the next few years' worth of investigations, and after it leaves Villisca, it never acts up like this again.

Erik and I remain downstairs, hanging out in the kitchen and taking a snack break, while Stephen heads up to the second floor to go check on some equipment. We suddenly hear quite the commotion coming from the top of the stairs. Before either of us can make it up there, Stephen comes on down, wearing a look of genuine surprise.

"What?" Erik and I both want to know.

Reaching for a bottle of water and taking a sip, Stephen tells us his story. He was standing in the master bedroom, with his back to the top of the staircase. Right at the top of the stairs, the lads have placed a device known as a Paramid

— a posh name for what is basically an ultra-sonic sensor, something which uses reflected sound waves to locate the presence of a physical object of some sort. According to the manufacturer, the Paramid is capable of detecting anything entering its sensor field for up to four feet in front or on either side.

"It uses the same sensors that are in a car bumper," Erik explains. Stephen nods in agreement.

"So anyway," he continues, "all of a sudden, the Paramid went off. It sounded an alarm. I was well out of range, so I knew somebody had to be standing right there that I couldn't see. And that's when the air conditioner switched itself on..."

Now *that's* impressive. I was very familiar with the two AC units at Villisca. Short of a massive power surge which would almost certainly have blown a fuse anyway, the only way to switch them on was to push a fairly stiff button on the front control panel. That would have taken a decent amount of force, especially if it was being applied by some kind of paranormal entity.

More electrical shenanigans in the Villisca Axe Murder House. Just what the doctor ordered.

An electronic warble from upstairs makes us all look up.

"That's the Paramid," Stephen says.

"Is it still at the top of the stairs?" Erik wants to know.

"Kind of. I moved it slightly, so it's next to Mr. and Mrs.

Moore's bed."

In other words, someone or something solid is standing next to the bed in the master bedroom. We troop upstairs, one after the other, with Stephen leading the way. The bedroom is, of course, completely deserted.

Something inside this house is playing games with us, just as Johnny Houser had said it would.

Erik sneezes. "Don't mind me," he sniffs. "I'm just allergic to Iowa."

When it comes to the paranormal field, one of my personal foibles is that I like to watch an episode or two of a TV show that was filmed at a haunted location while I am actually there. Of the multitude of so-called reality shows that are out there, one of my absolute favorites is *Ghost Lab*. This show, which first aired in the United States on the Discovery Channel in 2009, is one of the few to have gotten almost everything right. It's a show that died before its time.

In case you're not familiar with it, *Ghost Lab* stars Texas-based brothers Brad and Barry Klinge, along with their team-mates from Everyday Paranormal. Brad is, it's safe to say, the louder and more boisterous of the two, and is usually the point man when it comes to antagonizing some of the more negative spirits the brothers encounter. I'm going to say that Barry is the good-looking one, purely because I like to keep my life interesting, and by the time I finally get back to Texas, I'll have forgotten that I wrote this, and I'll be frantically trying to remember why Brad is so set on kicking my ass all the way to San Antonio and back.

The Klinges are pragmatists at heart. They hold no truck with bullshit or flim-flam, and always call it like it is. Sometimes that can be about as welcome as a bucket of cold water over the head, but quite often the brothers provide the kind of reality check that the field sorely needs. Knowing them both personally, I trust Brad and Barry's integrity implicitly. There's no showmanship or posing involved. If the Klinges say that a haunting is legitimate, then it's legitimate.

All of which made me even more excited to come to Villisca. Their episode of *Ghost Lab* (season 2, episode 10: *Path of a Killer*) contains some extraordinary evidence, and some fascinating insight into the case.

Setting up my trusty iPad in the middle of the parlor, I wait for Stephen and Erik to find a comfortable seat. Before they've gotten settled, my finger slips, and I start the episode a moment too early.

Apologizing under my breath, I stop the video and restart it when my colleagues are ready. It will only be later, when I review the audio recording, that I will realize something very unusual has just taken place.

There's no preamble to this episode — as the show opens, we're straight into Brad and Barry walking into the house. The brothers wander around the house by flashlight. Every reflective surface is already covered, just as they were on the night of the murders. Heading upstairs to the master bedroom, the beam of their light picks out the scuff marks on the wall which were caused by the back-swing of the killer's axe.

"They say the spirits here are pissed off," growls Brad, stalking around the attic as best he can with the low ceiling. "Just wait until they get a load of us..."

The *Ghost Lab* boys don't do the softly-softly approach. They're always willing to provoke, a technique that I'm not overly fond of myself except under very specific circumstances. For example, when I was investigating the John Wayne Gacy haunting of the R Theater in Auburn, Illinois, I had no qualms at all about provoking the spirit of a serial killer. I'm also wise enough to know that when it comes to provocation, it pays to involve the master. To that end, Brad video-conferenced in and gave Gacy's ghost a blistering mouthful of invective, the likes of which would have made the holy water in a font boil. (I'd normally say that it would have made a sailor blush, but Barry *was* a sailor in the US Navy, and he rarely bats an eye when Brad gets going).

On TV, however, the Klinges are a little more restrained.

We get some background on the case, courtesy of narrator and *Dirty Jobs* star Mike Rowe, including a run-down on some of the prime suspects. Team researcher Katie Burr emphasizes that people have been physically attacked inside the house by an unseen force. Chris Dedman recounts his experience for the Everyday Paranormal team too. A local resident claims that she was "hit from behind and pushed onto the floor.

The star witness is, of course, Johnny Houser, who sits down for an interview with Barry in the parlor. He relates the experience of three women who came one day to tour the house. One of the ladies poked her head into the closet in the children's bedroom, and as Johnny watched, suddenly recoiled as if pushed...which was, she said, exactly what had happened. It had felt to her as if a hand her pushed her on the head, causing her to stagger backward.

It sent a very unequivocal message: *you're not welcome here.*

To compound matters further, she felt her back beginning to burn. Lifting up her shirt, her companions were shocked to discover three scratch marks running across her back — just like Chris Dedman.

Johnny Houser shows a photograph of the unfortunate lady's injury. Three angry-looking bright red scars run in parallel across the right side of her back. They're most intense at the midline of her spine, gradually tapering off as they extend laterally toward the right side of her posterior chest. The scratches appear too thick to have been inflicted by the average human fingernail.

"I honestly think it knows what you guys are here for, and I don't think it really likes it too much," Johnny tells Barry.

Rather than employ psychic mediums and the metaphysical side of things, *Ghost Lab* is an extremely practical, tech-driven show. The brothers rely primarily on equipment and attitude in order to get things done.

A number of people have made the claim that the Villisca Axe Murder House is haunted by the spirit of the killer. It's a contention that has never made a great deal of sense to me. We know for certain that the murderer did not die at the house — indeed, if some students of the case are correct, may not have died in the town of Villisca itself. Why, then, would he haunt the house?

In response to this, Brad floats the theory that if a person is connected to a crime, sometimes they might be able to return to the scene of that crime. There may be some merit to this. I investigated the home of Herbert Baumeister, the serial killer once dubbed 'The I-70 Strangler,' at which he had murdered at least ten and possibly as many as nineteen or twenty victims (for full details, please see my book *The Horrors of Fox Hollow Farm*). Baumeister's presence has been sensed at the house by several witnesses, and his apparition has been reported there on more than one occasion. Baumeister didn't die at Fox Hollow Farm; he shot himself in the head on a beach in a Canadian national park. But he was connected with the house on a deep emotional level.

Why, then, should the same not be true of Villisca?

At this point, the Klinges introduce one of the most contentious facets of paranormal research: the electromagnetic field, or EMF. Electromagnetic fields can be generated artificially, by devices such as TVs, microwave ovens, refrigerators, and cell phones, but they can also occur naturally, in the human body and in the environment around it. Everyday Paranormal uses a series of EMF data loggers, devices which are capable of sensing changes in the strength of an electromagnetic field and charting it over a given span of time.

Believing that spirits manifest as a form of energy, Brad posits that one of those forms of energy might be electromagnetic. This was a very popular school of thought in the late 2000s and immediately before, when thousands of paranormal enthusiasts went out and bought their own K2 EMF meter, convinced that the device was some form of 'ghost detector.' Although there may indeed be a link between paranormal activity and EMF levels, it really isn't as simple as that. This is just my personal opinion, but I do not believe that ghosts necessarily give off or generate an electromagnetic field. However, I think it entirely possible that they might be able to affect a field that is already in existence, in the same way that a ship passing through the water might leave a wake behind it to mark its passing.

It is also entirely possible that spirit entities might be able to use EMF as an energy source, viewing a pre-existing EMF field in the same way that we would look at a free banquet: as a means to a greater end.

My preference when investigating is to use EMF meters to check the baseline levels of electromagnetic energy inside the haunted location, pinpointing the hot spots such as fluorescent lighting or the utility power lines coming into the house. The Klinges take this one step further. Rather than simply establishing a baseline, taking a snapshot at a single, specific point in time, their data loggers provide continuous tracking of EMF strength throughout the course of their investigation. EMF fields are dynamic, especially when they are influenced by something that the paranormal investigator can neither see nor understand.

"Let's just data log this house to death," Brad instructs his fellow team members in what may not be the most sensitive of phrasing, but definitely gets the point across. "Let's just put everything we got in there as far as loggers, and really analyze that too."

Team members will be monitoring the telemetry feed from the data loggers in real time, which should clue the boys in to anything strange that might be going on. It's a solid and innovative plan, and one that to my knowledge, nobody had tried at Villisca prior to the *Ghost Lab* episode. It may not have been repeated since, either.

Although the entire house is going to receive coverage, particular emphasis is given to the second floor, due to 75% of the murders having taken place up there. The investigation kicks off with an audio session. The Klinges are using an RT EVP recorder, a type of digital voice recorder which allows the speaker to listen to what's being recorded and pick up on potential EVPs as and when they come in. Brad Klinge is well-known for calling out the words *"mark it!"* when he hears what might be an EVP coming across his feed.

Brad and Barry make an appeal to Mr and Mrs Moore, and also to the children, but get nothing in the way of results. Then Brad switches gears, segueing into what he does best — provoking the killer himself.

Barry's in the attic, asking the killer if that's where he hid. The Ghost Lab technician radios to inform him that one of the EMF meters just spiked significantly. The meter is located in the children's bedroom closet. Then it spikes again. And again.

Sweat is streaming down Brad's face. Later, he will tell me that the house was so hot and devoid of air flow that the crew were forced to take a break that night and go back to the hotel for a while in order to cool off. This adds further credence to the observation that doors opening and closing by themselves inside the house are not being blown by wind.

Then a meter positioned on one of the children's beds goes off. More EMF spikes start to pop up on meters and data loggers all over the place.

The Villisca Axe Murder House is starting to come alive.

The Ghost Lab itself is a large trailer hauled by a truck. Inside, it is kitted out with some of the latest and greatest electronic sensing, monitoring, and display equipment. The Klinges and their team-mates begin plotting the EMF spikes from their meters and data loggers on a digital blueprint of the house.

The first spike came at 11:10 pm in the second-floor bedroom closet. It was a followed by a second three minutes later at 11:13, picked up by the sensor in the baby's crib.

Things start to get eerie when the data loggers located on the children's beds begin to fire off in a round-robin fashion. There are beds pushed against each one of the walls. Starting with the first bed, at 11:15, there's an EMF spike. Another comes at 11:19 on the bed next to it, followed by yet another on the final remaining bed at 11:22.

The EMF spikes all come at three to four-minute intervals, following a specific track from the closet, to the crib, and passing through all three of the children's beds.

As if that wasn't crazy enough, three minutes later, the sensors in the master bedroom begin alarming at 11:25.

All this has to be coincidence...right?

Except that five minutes later, the EMF data logger in the downstairs bedroom — the room in which the Stillinger children were murdered — is set off.

Every single one of those EMF spikes occurs in the specific place where a victim was killed by the Villisca Axeman.

Looking at the pattern a little more closely, it's hard (if not impossible) to avoid coming to the same conclusion that the Klinges do. If the killer walked from bed to bed, murdering each of the occupants in turn, then the path he took would look a lot like the layout of the EMF spikes recorded on the data loggers.

A lot.

The only discrepancy that I can see is the sequence. The killer is believed to have been hiding in the attic. If had waited until the Moore family and their guests were asleep before emerging from his hideout, then it would have made sense for him to turn right and kill Josiah and Sara Moore first — as adults, they were obviously the greatest threat. Of the two, Josiah, the male, was the greater cause for concern, which is why he was almost certainly attacked first by the axe man. Sara Moore, and all of the other children, were almost certainly bludgeoned to death afterward, when the Axeman felt a little more secure.

If the killer had instead been lurking in the closet and had murdered the Moore children first, then he would have run the risk of waking their parents, and having to deal with two adults who were fighting for their lives. That means that although the Klinges' sensors could well have captured the path of the killer, I believe that the sequence could have been incorrect. It does make sense that the murders of the Stillinger girls in the downstairs bedroom would have happened last, however, and the *Ghost Lab* team have captured some truly thought-provoking evidence.

Of course, it should also be born in mind that the first EMF spike came from the closet, a closet whose door has been observed to open and close itself of its own accord on numerous occasions. *something* definitely isn't right with that particular part of the building.

There is also no guarantee that the adults were killed first. It is likely that we will never know for sure, so it is entirely possible that the killer — who was almost certainly not of sound mind at the time, because just *look* at what he did — was behaving irrationally anyway. It may well be a serious mistake to project any kind of intelligence onto the behavior of a homicidal maniac.

Could the Klinges really have captured the energy "footprint" of the Villisca Axeman? They hope to find out more on night two.

The weather could not have been more perfect. It truly is a dark and stormy night when the Klinge Brothers make their way across the lawn for a second evening of investigation. Jagged forks of electric blue lightning flashes against the dark sky, one of those long, rolling thunderstorms that Iowans know all too well.

Tonight, Brad is not playing around. Hefting an axe in his left hand — remember that the killer is also believed to have been left-handed — he addresses him directly. He floats the theory that the killer was hiding not in the attic but in the children's closet, then came out of hiding when they were asleep.

"I can only imagine that the parents woke up by this time," he booms, pacing the room while Barry videos the proceedings. "You moved to their bedroom. You kill. You kill the other one. Then you go downstairs—" Brad descends, still hefting the axe, and stops by the guest room, indicating that the two Stillinger daughters were murdered there. "—and then you silently slip off into the night."

Laying the axe down carefully, resting the handle against

the wall, Brad circles the confines of the kitchen. "Why'd you do it, man? Why?"

Suddenly, he stiffens. Apparently, he hears something through the RT-EVP earpiece. "Mark time. *Mark it.* Male voice."

Amazingly, he has gotten a direct answer.

The EVP is clear, and somewhere between a Class B+ and Class A in quality — close to the gold standard.

"Why'd you do it, man? Why?"

For fun.

The voice is breathy, hushed, and sinister. Very clearly male. It plainly isn't a member of the Everyday Paranormal team.

They asked, and the answer was given.

The following morning, the Klinges present their evidence to Johnny Houser. He finds their presentation impressive, calling them "huge pieces to the puzzle." I suspect that he is one hundred percent right.

There's an eerie coda to the *Ghost Lab* story, albeit one that would not take place until several years after the episode had aired. Long after the Klinge Brothers had packed up their gear and taken the Lab back to Texas, another paranormal team was spending the night at the Moore House, conducting their own research.

Much to their surprise, they recorded the sound of a loud, booming male voice, barking out two very distinctive words:

Mark it!

The implications of this are fascinating and wide-ranging. "Mark it!" is, of course, the ultimate Brad Klinge-ism, something that he would say on a frequent and regular basis, and something that is virtually unique to him. Brad is thankfully not dead at the time of writing (at least, he wasn't when I spoke to him an hour ago) and so we can rule out the possibility of his spirit, soul, call it whatever you will, haunting the Villisca Axe Murder House.

The other possibilities are equally intriguing, however. Even the most mundane paranormal explanation — that Brad's voice was somehow recorded during his visit, and imprinted on the atmosphere or the structure in some way — is fascinating. This would qualify as being a residual phenomenon, capable of being picked up and replayed under the right conditions at a future time. But it's equally possible that this wasn't Brad speaking at all; rather, some kind of time-slip event might have occurred. Far-fetched, I would agree, but no less impossible for that.

It could also be that an entity inside the house was mimicking Brad, making fun of him in its own way. The man has certainly made enemies during the course of his career in the paranormal research field, many of whom are not among the living. No matter what the answer may be, it's almost impossible to dismiss this as being nothing more than a coincidence. It seems that Brad Klinge has left his own indelible imprint in the energies of the Villisca Axe Murder House.

Remember how I accidentally started the video a few seconds too early, then had to stop it and re-start it from the beginning? It was only during the audio review phase that I finally realized I had captured something bizarre, a noise overlaid on top of the video soundtrack. In other words, an EVP.

The EVP sounds like a young child giggling. It almost seems to be laughing at me for screwing up and starting the video too early. Certainly, there are no children in the house — right now, there are just three middle-aged men. There are also no kids playing in the street outside or on the lawn behind the house. We check all of the windows, just to make sure.

So where had the childish giggle come from?

I'm suddenly reminded of the *Ghost Adventures* episode, in which the two women who had lived in this house and slept in this very same room had reported hearing the sound of a little girl crying. The parallels are not lost on me. In both cases, we have an auditory phenomenon — in my case, an EVP, and in theirs, direct voice phenomenon. Both of them are childish in nature, from the sound of them. Could they have the same root cause, or at the very least, a similar explanation? Because if not, I'll have to try and accept that it's a huge coincidence, and that's not an answer I'm ready to buy into just yet.

After I stop the video, the three of us sit and relax in the parlor for a while. Intermittently, throughout the screening of *Ghost Lab*, we'd hear the sound of the Paramid going off in the master bedroom upstairs.

About halfway through, Stephen had disappeared, returning two minutes later and explaining that he'd gone to set a digital voice recorder running in the hopes of catching anything the unseen visitor might say.

"That damn Paramid has been going off all through the TV show," Erik grumbles. Stephen disagrees.

"No, it hasn't. It stopped when I went up there with the recorder."

As if on cue, we can suddenly hear the Paramid bleeping, calling out to us from upstairs. We look at one another as if to say, *What perfect timing.*

"I'm suddenly not comfortable turning my back to that stairway," Stephen tells us. That raises an eyebrow. Over the past ten years, I have spent many nights with Stephen in some of the most darkly haunted, negative places imaginable; prisons, abandoned hospitals, even murder sites. I've never seen him unnerved like this before. To be clear, he's far from terrified, just somewhat on edge, but considering some of the things we have seen and experienced together, that by itself is quite unusual.

One of the best ways to deal with fear is, of course, to confront it head on, and that's exactly what we propose to do next. Thus far, nobody has ever gained any useful intelligence as to the identity of the Villisca Axe Murderer, and while I'm not optimistic about our chances, we all agree that it's worth at least giving it a try.

With multiple voice recorders running, Stephen starts to ask a series of very pointed questions.

"Who is the murderer?" he begins. "Are the family members and their two guests at peace? Is the murderer condemned? What is the name of the murderer? Who carried out this heinous act? Who takes responsibility for this?"

Another train rumbles by in the distance, its horn bellowing. It doesn't break the priest's concentration.

"Will you ever be able to leave? Who was standing in the doorway earlier?"

In the perfect world — or if this was a movie, set in, say,

The Conjuring universe — then we would end up with an EVP giving us the name of the killer. In reality, we had no such luck. On playback, nobody deigned to answer any of Stephen's questions. That's pretty much what we were expecting, but there's still an air of slight disappointment nevertheless.

Next, we decide to focus on the Moore children's bedroom upstairs, splitting our time between the beds and the closet. Once again, our burst EVP sessions do not bear fruit. Outside in the street, two of the neighborhood stray cats get into a fight, hissing and clawing at one another, but beyond that, all is peaceful and quiet.

"We haven't tried the attic yet," Stephen suggests. Indeed, we haven't. It takes no small amount of squeezing and pushing for the three of us to get in there. Once we do, we take up positions sitting in a circle on the bare floorboards. Despite the range of toys scattered about the place, our EVP questions are directed toward the killer, based purely on the premise that he is believed to have hidden in here on the night of the murders. Unlike the Klinges, I've never believed that he would have cause to haunt the scene of his crime, although I could buy the possibility that his spirit might come back to visit and relive his sick and twisted handiwork. Still, it comes as no surprise that all of our questions are met with silence.

With the attic also being a bust, we make our way to the

master bedroom for the next session. Despite the antics of the Paramid earlier on, nobody's talking in here either. The same is true of the staircase, the kitchen, and the downstairs bedroom. The atmosphere feels flat to us, as if whatever was here earlier has already left.

We're all stifling yawns, and sunrise isn't far away. We give it one last shot, hooking up a spirit box in the parlor and settling down for one last experiment. I've recently brought a brand-new, custom-built spirit box, and brought it along with me to try it out. After a few seconds spent fiddling with the controls, I have the room filled with the hiss of static and white noise. The problem is, the bloody thing refuses to change its sweep. The frequency-hopping controller worked just fine at home, when I tested it out prior to packing it in Styrofoam before making the long drive to Iowa. Now, it's stuck on the same radio frequency and flatly refuses to budge.

After a few minutes of attempted troubleshooting, which primarily involves cursing under my breath and slapping the side of the box, I give up. It's getting late — or rather, getting early — and we're all tired. It's time for us to caffeinate and hit the road.

Packing up our equipment, we load up the car and give the house one last sweep. Stephen and Eric agree that the energies which had played cat and mouse with us earlier have dissipated. Whatever was here at the start of the night has gone...for now.

A few days after we get back to Colorado, my new spirit box still refuses to sweep. I continue to turn the dial, and nothing happens. I shrug, writing it off as a simple mechanical or electrical malfunction, but email the builder anyway to let him know what happened.

His reply pops into my inbox later that day.

"You were just at Villisca, weren't you? What the hell is it with that place? You're the third person who has had one of my boxes go crazy in that house. It doesn't happen anywhere else."

I'm sitting in my office on a Sunday afternoon, going over the photographs from our night of investigation there. One of them contains something unusual. It's a photograph that I took of the digital screen in Erik's car, showing the GPS address and directions to the Villisca Axe Murder House. My phone is clearly visible, reflected on the screen, from the moment at which the picture had been taken. But there is something else.

A face. No, scratch that: a face and a head. A *horned*

head. It looks, for all intents and purposes, like the Devil.

As things turn out, there's a very simple explanation, and one that Erik is able to clear up in seconds. What I'm looking at is, in fact, the face of a demon. The Dodge Demon, logo of the automobile manufacturer, to be precise. It's one of the background wallpapers on his car's UConnect infotainment system. I hadn't noticed it at the time I took the photo, but a simple side-by-side comparison of the logo and my photograph proves it.

Some so-called anomalies are easy to debunk. Other strange things end up being something else entirely, as we will learn when we decide to go back to Villisca for one last investigation.

CHAPTER FOURTEEN
"The House Knows You're Coming."

Whatever else you might say about the Villisca Axe Murder House, one thing is undeniably true: there's just something about the place that just sucks you right back in. Which is why I found myself heading back there once again, in the company of several different friends and fellow paranormal investigators.

It's a clear, hot summer afternoon when I return to Villisca again. I'm about seven hours into the drive when my phone pings, alerting me to an incoming text. Glancing down, I see that it's from Johnny Houser. I pull into the next gas station to get a bottle of water and check what it says.

Hey, buddy. The atmosphere inside the house is really strange today. It's even making me uncomfortable. I think the house knows you're coming.

That sends a splash of ice water running through my veins. If Johnny Houser, Mister Villisca himself, is feeling weirded out, and thinks that it's because the house knows that I'm coming to stay, then...oh, crap. That does not sound good.

Lost in thought, I wander into the gas station and pay for my drink. Just as I'm leaving, my phone pings again.

People are leaving the hours in tears today. Also, a kid got grabbed by something on one of the tours. Just FYI.

Oh, that's just great. So, nothing to worry about, then...

Stephen and Erik weren't able to make it this trip, but I've brought along four other trusted investigators. I've worked with all of them before, and in addition to being absolutely confident of their abilities, I'm wondering whether increasing the number of people who are present in the house this time will also ramp up the level of paranormal activity. After all, we'll be adding significantly more energy into the mix.

Jason and I go way back. Originally an East Coaster, he and his wife Linda relocated to Colorado a few years ago, and formed their own paranormal research team. We soon became firm friends, and it's a rarity these days when at least one of them isn't on an investigation with me. He's shorter than the average bear, bald, with a neatly-trimmed beard and an expression of near-constant intensity whenever he's deep in thought.

Charlie and I both worked for the same private ambulance company; he as an EMT, and me as a paramedic. I like having another medical professional around, and he's a solid paranormal investigator to boot. Charlie's a few steps ahead of me in the thinning hair stakes, and despite being of medium stature, he's more than capable of restraining a combative patient when the need arises.

Catlyn's our resident academic, with a PhD and many years' experience in teaching comparative religions. If there's a theological question, she's our go-to source. She's an expert in how the multitude of global cultures approach the subject of God, death, and the role of gender. Catlyn's at home every bit as much on the back of a speeding motorbike as she is in the classroom.

Lastly, but by no means least, Sarah is also back for this one. She's well acquainted with the house and the haunting, and will be our designated photographer for the investigation.

I'm proud to count all of them as my personal friends, in addition to being colleagues in good standing. It's a true friend indeed that will make a thousand-mile road trip in order to help you investigate a haunted Axe Murder House, after all, and I'm fully aware of how lucky I am to number these guys as part of my circle.

Sarah and I have been here before, as has Jason, along with his wife, Linda. They captured some interesting EVPs during their last visit, including a Class A recording of a woman's voice saying the words *Do not enter.*

Our little convoy arrives at the Moore House late in the afternoon, and we all park outside. We're met at the barn door by a grinning Johnny Houser. After a round of hearty greetings for those of us who already know him, he leads the newcomers into the house while Jason and I make for the barn in order to sign for the house.

Meeting Martha Linn, the owner of the house, is a very

enjoyable experience. Previously, I've only ever seen her on TV, most notably interviewed by *The Dead Files'* Steve DiSchiavi.

I'm glad to find that Martha is one of those people who is completely without any pretensions. What you see on TV is exactly what you get when you meet her in person. When I walk into the office at the back of the barn, I find her sitting behind the counter, taking care of some paperwork. After a short while, we're chatting away like old friends.

Once she heads home for the night, I go into the house in order to catch up with Johnny. As soon as the kitchen door closes behind me, I feel as if I'm picking up on the strange atmosphere that he warned me about earlier on that day. It feels as if something really *is* off about the house; then again, my skeptical brain points out, Johnny's text has already predisposed me toward thinking something was up here. Maybe what I'm feeling is nothing more than my own subconscious making me feel exactly what it is that I'm expecting to feel.

While the rest of my team is exploring the house, the first-timers moving excitedly from one room to the next, I take Johnny aside and ask him to tell me exactly what happened on the tour earlier that day. "It was a history tour. No ghosts," he says. "Then this kid, he had to have been about ten years old, just starts bawling and runs out of the house. When we finally get him to calm down, he tells us that something grabbed him on the leg."

I let out a low whistle. That's something that would shake up any ten-year-old.

"Even *I've* been tearing up all day," Johnny adds, shaking his head. "There's just such a sense of sadness in there today. "

After chatting for a little while longer, he takes his leave and heads back home, leaving the five of us in possession of the house. The first thing we do is check all the doors and windows, then search the place from top to bottom, in order to make sure that everything's secure. It is. Finally satisfied, we all congregate in the living room.

It's hot without the AC running. Everybody is sweating already, clothes sticking to our bodies in a host of unpleasant ways, but we decide to forego the luxury of cold air for a little while longer so that we can get used to the feeling of the house.

Odd things are already beginning to happen. The batteries in Jason's TASCAM, a top of the range digital audio recorder, are already drained, despite being fully charged when he first came into the house. That cheers me up straight away. Unexplained power drains are often a precursor of paranormal activity. It's almost as if the energy is being converted into a different form, some kind of state that spirits can use for their own purposes.

In the hope of energizing things a little bit, we settle

down to enjoy a cold drink and watch the episode of *Kindred Spirits* that was shot in the house. Unlike the *Ghost Lab* episode, there are no EVPs of little children giggling this time. My crew provides a constant running commentary, in the style of *Mystery Science Theater 3000*.

By the time it's over, it's starting to get dark outside, casting the parlor into shadow. There's a definite sense of heaviness hanging over the house, almost as if it's holding its breath. Even I'm able to feel it, and there are rocks in the River Thames that are more sensitive to this stuff than I am.

We fire off a quick burst EVP session, with Sarah leading the way.

"Is there anybody in here with us?" she begins, pointing to the array of voice recorders we have clustered in the center of the parlor. "If you want to talk to us, you can talk into one of these devices."

And suddenly, we're hearing voices. Unfortunately, they come not from ghosts, but rather from two very chatty old ladies standing across the street. It's a windless summer's evening, which means that just like the ubiquitous train horns, their voices are being carried on the still night air.

This unexpected piece of noise contamination puts paid to our burst session, so we retreat further into the house, taking up residence in the Stillinger sisters' bedroom. This time, I take the lead, asking questions about the unfortunate ghost hunter who stabbed himself in this room. Who had done it? For what reason?

When I play the recording back, there are no answers. Just the far-off drone of two local residents talking about whatever it is one talks about in the street outside an axe murder house of an evening.

A third session in the kitchen, led by Jason, is a little more interesting. He goes all-out after the killer. "Come on, you piece of shit," he booms. "You did something horrific in this house. 'Fess up to it."

Apparently, somebody does. A male voice whispers something immediately after Jason tells them to fess up. Unfortunately, this is at best a Class C EVP, which means that although it is most definitely a whispering voice, it's extremely difficult to tell exactly what is being said, even after it has been digitally cleaned up and enhanced.

Still, it looks as if somebody might be in the mood to talk to us.

"Why did you do it? Did you have any help?" Other than Jason's voice, the kitchen is silent. Even the two conversationalists outside have suddenly gone quiet. "Did you know this family before you came here that day — or that night? Was this an act of revenge, or a crime of opportunity?"

No more EVPs show up. Just getting one is cause for cautious optimism. Our next stop is the attic. Jason gets a ration of crap because he's a little on the short side and doesn't have to duck like the rest of us ("hey, you can just walk straight in!"). Catlyn takes point, speaking with a very firm tone of voice that, I imagine, can turn the bowels of her college students to ice water if they haven't completed an assignment on time.

She addresses the negative entity we've heard so much about from Johnny and other visitors.

"I hear that there's something in this house that really doesn't like being called out. Something that feeds on fear. *I'm* not afraid of you." Catlyn is not a woman given to fear. She looks around the attic, peering into every shadow. Her questions go unanswered when we play back the audio. Nothing is biting up here, either literally or figuratively.

Charlie leads the next session, still in the attic. He tries to connect with any children that might be present (hopefully none, in my opinion) asking about their favorite games and whether they have any brothers and sisters. It's a novel approach, but unfortunately one that also fails to yield any fruit. The attic seems, for want of a better word, dead...

...until, that is, Catlyn begins to feel an ice-cold draft shooting down the left side of her body. It's strong enough for her to mention it to us. In the cramped confines of the attic, with five of us crammed in there, Catlyn is the only one feeling a chill. The rest of us just *wish* we could. The AC is still off, and we're sweltering in there. There's not even a hint of a breeze coming in from any tiny gaps there might be around the window frame. Four of us are sweating like mad, and Catlyn is beginning to shiver. There *is* some very slight air movement, but not enough to move a small piece of paper, and what air there is, is coming in from outside — which means it's tepid, not ice cold. It's Iowa in July, not November.

I think back to the visitor log entries I read. A number of people reported experiencing the same thing. Crucially, Catlyn hasn't read them — I know this because they're still locked in the barn — and therefore shouldn't be influenced by them. Which makes what's happening to her all the more interesting. Could it be paranormal? Perhaps. It could also just be the warm outside air giving her gooseflesh.

The attic is starting to feel a little close, so we head to the only room we haven't looked at yet — the Moore children's bedroom. Jason runs this burst session. He's a dad, and has a good rapport with kids, so he's one of the obvious choices to try connecting with the children. If there are the spirits of children around, they're keeping themselves to themselves. For me, at least, that's good news. I hate the possibility of those kids still hanging around after all these years.

That's it. We've now covered the whole house with burst EVP work, and gotten one partial result for our trouble. It's time to get a little more targeted. We file downstairs to the parlor. No sooner have we arrived than there's a knock coming from the Stillinger bedroom behind us. The air conditioning unit in there is off, so there's nothing with which to account for it. Yet several of us hear it.

We wait quietly in the parlor for a while, but nothing else happens. It's decided that we'll trying a talking board up in the attic. Although some might have aversions to using such a method in a place like this, I'm confident that as long as we open and close it properly, and employ adequate psychic protection before we leave, then everything will work out fine.

Back in the attic, everybody settles to the floor with a series of creaks and groans that are about fifty percent floorboards, fifty percent middle-aged bones and joints. The board is placed carefully on the floor in the center of the room, with a planchette on top. It's fully dark outside now, and the lack of electric lighting means we have to use a flashlight to illuminate it. To rule out bias as much as possible, we also blindfold the participants.

Catlyn opens up the board, stressing that we will only work with positive, honest, and decent spirit entities. None others are permitted to communicate via the board. She has two fingers on the planchette, along with Charlie and Sarah. It does not move at first, until Catlyn encourages any potential communicators to think of it "like playing a game with us." When she says that, the planchette suddenly shoots off the edge of the board.

We're off to the races.

"Slide it around," Catlyn says, moving the planchette to the center of the board herself. She asks for the communicator to place it over the number which matches up with its age. The planchette obligingly slides over to the number seven. My eyebrows shoot up. Arthur Moore, also known as Boyd, was seven years old when he died, just ten feet or so to my right.

"Are you a girl? A female?" she continues. The planchette slides toward NO but once again takes a dive bomb off the edge of the board. Catlyn replaces it. "Are you a boy?" No response. "Are you human?" Nothing.

She moves the planchette in a series of figure-eights around the board, with the intent of building up a little energy. "Are you a girl?" she repeats. The answer is also NO. Are we really communicating with the spirit of a seven-year-old boy, I wonder, or are we dealing with some trickster, despite Catlyn's statement of intent to the contrary? With a talking board, one never quite knows for sure. Especially in this place.

Now, everything suddenly grinds to a halt. The planchette stops moving. Ten minutes later, it's still as dead as a dodo. Frustrated, we pack up the board and head back to the bedroom where the Moore children were killed, and set it up in there. It's still open, so Catlyn gets straight down to business, asking if there are any willing communicators available to speak with us.

Yes, is the immediate answer. Once again, when asked its age, the planchette goes right back to the number seven.

"Is this the same entity we were just communicating with in the attic?"

Yes.

Now the unseen communicator claims to be a little boy.

"Please move to the first letter of your name."

The planchette slides across to T.

"Is your name Thomas, by any chance?" Catlyn asks. YES, comes the answer. "Huh. What are the odds I would have guessed that?"

"Because it's the most popular male T-name in the English-speaking world?" Jason posits, bursting her bubble. Catlyn nods, admitting that he's absolutely right. Is this simply her own subconscious at play?

In the distance, another train sounds its horn.

Catlyn wants to know whether she's really talking to a spirit entity or just playing mind games with herself. Fortunately, we have a standard test to help determine just that.

"Do the fingers thing," she tells me. Surreptitiously, I place my hands behind my back and stick up six fingers. Jason takes a photo with his camera, capturing my hands squarely in frame.

"The gentleman over there has raised a number of

fingers behind his back," Catlyn announces. "If you can see how many, please let us know."

Instantly, the planchette is in motion.

"What number is that?" Jason asks.

"Six," she repeats. "How many fingers do you have up." I raise my hands.

"Six."

"NO WAY!" Catlyn's taken aback. There is a one-in-ten chance that she could have randomly guessed the number, but those aren't great gambling odds. "Thank you for doing that!"

Now it's Sarah's turn to sound a little skeptical. "Let's try this again. Richard is going to hold up a different number of fingers. Please tell us how many that is."

The planchette slides across the board again.

"Frickin' frackin' *nine*," Jason whistles, shaking his head in disbelief.

"Is that how many he's holding up?" Catlyn asks. He nods slowly, hardly able to believe what he's seeing. Another one-in-ten long shot comes up trumps.

Nobody seriously believes we're making it up ourselves.

"Did you live in this house?" Catlyn wants to know. *No,* comes the immediate answer. "Did you have a friend who lived here?" *No* again.

"Do you have anything to do with the house next door?" I interject, meaning the Houser family residence. The answer is *Yes*.

Catlyn asks if the communicator once lived there, and the response says that they did.

"Did you *die* in the house next door?" Jason asks, getting the answer *No*.

"Are you buried in the Villisca town cemetery?" Catlyn asks. The answer is a hesitant *Yes*. Things were looking promising, but when she tries to get Thomas to spell out his last name for us, the board stops working, and nothing we say can coax it back into life. It's almost as if we've gone a step too far by asking such a personal question.

After ten more wasted minutes, we finally admit defeat. "Where next?" I ask, looking around at the faces of my team mates. Sarah says that she'd like to try the Stillinger girls' bedroom, so that's where we go. Getting five of us in there is a bit crowded; one person has to sit in the closet. It's tight, but we all find a spot of our own. Sarah raises eyebrows by picking up a child's doll and putting it in her lap.

This next session is devoted to making contact with the little girls who are said to haunt this room. I keep thinking of Amy Allan's claim that one of them is a prankster, who likes nothing better than to give the living a good scare by growling at them.

"You know what would be really funny?" Catlyn says, apropos of nothing. "If you went and poked Richard in the back."

There's a murmur of general agreement. I present my back to the center of the room, turning to face the closet instead. The intent is to offer up an inviting target, but if so, nobody takes advantage of it.

We keep the mood jovial and light, partly because it should be more attractive to any child spirits, but also as an attempt to counteract the general air of negativity that pervades the house.

Suddenly, there's a low growl. For the first time all night, it isn't coming from somebody's stomach. Each investigator confirms that it wasn't one of us. The low rumble was short in duration, and seemed to come from somewhere in the center of the room, next to the bed.

Catlyn quickly breaks out the talking board, placing it on the bed. Once she opens it up, asks if the communicator would "like to play the number game again." The answer is a slow but definite *Yes*.

This time, however, the answer is wrong. The planchette selects the number zero, but I'm actually holding up five fingers behind my back. It's wrong the second time, too. Strange, when it had worked so well upstairs just a few minutes before.

"Are you intentionally lying to us about the fingers?" Catlyn asks. *No*, is the answer. "Is this still Thomas we're talking to?" *No*, again.

This communicator claims to be neither a boy nor a girl

— when Catlyn asks if it's human, the answer also comes back as no. Then she has an epiphany. "Are you the house? Is the house itself communicating with us?"

The planchette refuses to answer. Now *that's* interesting. Johnny Houser's theory, that the Villisca Axe Murder House may well be a rare case of a building actually haunting itself, is starting to look like a solid possibility.

She asks if the board can point to the first letter of her name, and is rewarded with the planchette moving to the letter C.

"Are you happy here, in this house?" Catlyn goes on. An unequivocal *No* comes back. I ask if it's possible for whoever it is to leave, and the planchette immediately flies off the board and falls onto the floor, passing over *Goodbye* as it goes.

We each look at one another in turn. That's quite the response. Catlyn picks it up and puts it in the center of the board. The instant that the participants rest their fingers on it again, it moves to *Goodbye*. And stays there.

"Well," Jason says. "That's pretty clear."

"So, we lost Thomas when we came down to the ground floor," I recap, "and then picked up somebody new in here. Not the Stillinger girls, of that we're sure; could we really have just been in communication with the energy of the Villisca Axe Murder House itself, somehow made manifest and quasi-intelligent? The possibility is a fascinating one, and has implications for the rest of the paranormal field which will require lots of analysis and consideration.

But why was it unable to answer the question regarding how many fingers I was holding up, something which the communicator named Thomas was able to do with complete accuracy not just once but twice in a row? The thought strikes me that, as ridiculous as it sounds, disembodied spirits have eyes and are able to see; actual *houses* do not. Could it really be that simple...or are we being played?

I feel as though the board has run its course, but Catlyn isn't ready to give up on it just yet. Charlie's arms are getting tired, so he asks me if I'll swap out with him. I'm only too happy to, taking his place on the bed and resting my index finger on the planchette. Sarah is still sitting on the floor with the creepy-looking doll in her lap, and Jason is filming us from the back of the room.

"Is there anybody here that wishes to communicate with us, please?" Catlyn asks. "Let us know that you're here." Catlyn asks. All eyes are on the planchette, but what happens next has nothing to do with it. Three loud, distinct raps sound on the wall just above the bed. They're as clear as if I had reached up one hand and rapped with my knuckles, *knock-knock-knock,* one after the other in rapid succession.

It's a holy shit moment. It wasn't any of the investigators — the video footage from Jason's camera proves that none of us were moving. Jason heads outside to check the exterior of the building, making sure there's nobody out there...which, of course, there isn't. He does a full three-sixty of the building, and finds it deserted. It's one of the best direct responses to a question that I've ever heard, solid knocks that were timed to perfection — a split-second after Catlyn asked for communication.

We're all blown away. This is one of those oh so rare, crystal clear instances of audible phenomena that every paranormal investigator so desperately craves. There's no way to write it off as being the house creaking or settling, water running through (nonexistent) pipes, or human agency. This was a paranormal response to Catlyn's request, perfectly timed and completely unexpected.

This is exactly why we do what we do.

Now that we have some momentum going, everybody agrees that we need to keep it up. We're still in the bedroom in which the Stillinger sisters were killed. Sarah takes over at the talking board, and soon ascertains that not only is something willing to talk with her, but that it also claims to be the same entity we were speaking with earlier.

She asks the one thing we're all thinking; whether this is the same entity that made the three knocks earlier. The planchette goes straight to *Goodbye* and refuses to budge, no matter what. We're frustrated, but grateful for the knocks we got. Catlyn closes down the board, and performs a short ritual to protect us all. Everybody feels better after that. You never want to take something home from a haunted location, but that goes double for *this* haunted location.

It's time to employ another technique, this time the so-called Estes Method. This involves placing a paranormal investigator in a state of sensory deprivation, by having them wear a blindfold and wearing a set of noise-canceling headphones. The headphones are hooked into a Spirit Box, which feeds the raw audio from its frequency-hopping sweeps directly into their ears, and their ears alone (though a splitter cable can hook the audio output into a digital voice recorder, for analysis later). The other investigators take turns to ask questions, and the hope is that answers come through the Spirit Box directly, without any intervening bias on the part of the listener.

It's an interesting technique, and one we've had moderate to great success with in the past. Charlie volunteers to go "under the hood," slipping on the blindfolds and headphone. We set the spirit box to a respectable sweep rate and start to ask questions that he cannot possibly hear.

The gist of our questions is whether the killer rode into town on the train, why he covered all of the mirrors and reflective surfaces, and what his state of mind was at the time of the murders. Unfortunately, none of Charlie's statements make any sense when taken in context. They're just a series of random words. We give it fifteen minutes, and then bring him back out into the light.

It's time for another break. As we're shooting the breeze and enjoying a snack, we plan our next move. It's been a long night so far, and everybody feels like doing something a little mindless. We decide to kick back in the parlor for a little while and re-watch the episode of *Ghost Adventures* that was shot here.

And that's when it happens.

A dog barks at us. It's not coming from my iPad — there is no barking dog in that particular episode of *Ghost Adventures* — and the bark is so loud, we're all convinced that it's right here in the room with us. Which is patently ridiculous, because the house is still locked up tight and there isn't a four-legged friend to be seen.

"Could it have been outside?" I ask doubtfully, absolutely convinced that it wasn't.

"Only one way to find out." Jason and Catlyn are already moving, heading for the door. I go to the window and push aside the curtain. I can see the street outside very clearly. There's no dog. Meanwhile, my colleagues are making a circuit of the house and its outbuildings, searching for a stray pooch. There's none in sight. When I get back home to Colorado the following day, I call Johnny and ask him if he can review the footage from the security cameras to tell us if we were visited by a dog at any point during the night. We never were.

Then it hits me: bloodhounds. When the bodies of the Moores and the Stillingers were found, and the hunt for the killer began, bloodhounds were brought to the house in an attempt to track him down. Was that what we had just heard, a residual after-echo of that long-ago day in 1912, when the trail which would ultimately go cold began right here, on this very spot?

That's the high point of the night. Following the bark, the energy in the house appears to subside just as quickly as it spiked. Charlie, Catlyn, and Sarah leave a little before sunrise, in order to get a jumpstart on the long drive home. Jason and I stick around a little while longer, just getting a feel for the place now that there are just two of us left.

A last couple of burst EVP sessions fail to turn up any anomalous voices, and the atmosphere inside the house has started to feel rather inert. Slowly, we pack our equipment away and load it up. It's been yet another noteworthy night at the Villisca Axe Murder House, yet so many questions still remain unanswered.

Who knocked on the wall of the Stillinger girls' bedroom? Who exactly was Thomas, and how much of what he told us was the truth – if anything? Were there any spirits in the house at all, or was this actually case of a house that's haunting itself? And lastly, did we really encounter a phantom dog, of all things?

I have a lot to think about on the long drive west. I lock the kitchen door and the screen door, then place the keys in a secure location for Johnny to retrieve later today. As Jason puts the car into drive and we hit the road, I stare at the house in the rear-view mirror until we turn the corner and it drops out of sight.

It's hard to shake the feeling that it's laughing at me, and at my arrogance in thinking I could possibly uncover all of its secrets.

CHAPTER FIFTEEN
Respect

Troy Taylor is a prolific, highly-regarded author in the genres of paranormal non-fiction, history, and folklore. He has made many visits to the Villisca Axe Murder House over the years, while researching his book *Murdered in Their Beds*, and has come to know both the case and the house in great detail. There are few people who understand the Villisca Axe Murders and their place in a broader context as Troy does, and he was gracious enough to sit down for an interview with me in order to share his experience and perspective.

My first question to him is whether he thinks we will ever know the identity of the perpetrator. He does not. "Many of the people in Villisca are still convinced that the killer was somebody local," Troy says, "but I don't see it that way. I think this was a serial killer, one who committed at least several other murders, but we'll never know for sure who that was."

The authors of *The Man From The Train* do reveal the identity of a suspect they believe to have been the murderer, but while both they and Troy agree that the Villisca Axe Murders were almost certainly carried out by a lone individual who came in on the railroad, Troy does not believe there is sufficient evidence to identify him.

"There *no possible way* we can know," he continues, warming to his theme. "This was a transient, traveling killer, who just stopped killing one day and disappeared. He most probably died, or was locked up for something else. He may even have ended up in an asylum. I don't have enough faith in the so-called 'paranormal messages' that come through, to tell us who the killer was. I just don't buy it. We're never going to get anything that we can accept as evidence by those methods."

I tend to agree with him, not least because results obtained by different paranormal investigators have turned out to be confusing at best and even downright contradictory.

"Whoever the killer was, do you think that he watched the family enter the house from the barn and then broke in after they had gone to bed," I ask him, "or do you believe that he was there waiting for them, hiding in the attic all along?"

"I've never ruled out the attic possibility," Troy responds, "but I believe he broke in after they were all asleep. I can't say for sure if he was hiding in the barn, but I do believe that he arrived on the train earlier in the day, and had already chosen the house he wanted to target beforehand. He was spotted earlier in the day, wandering around town. Remember that back in those days, *nobody* locked their door, especially in small towns like Villisca.

There was very little crime. Hank Horton [the town marshal] spent most of his time locking up drunks and breaking up fights. I've come to suspect that the killer was able to just walk into the house and commit the murders after the lights were out."

"Do you think he went up to the second floor and killed the adults first, or were the Stillinger girls killed in the downstairs bedroom before that?" I ask.

"I base my answer to that question on the other Midwest Axe Murders. He *always* killed the man first, or any adult, because he had to get the biggest threat out of the way. There was no way he was ever going to walk into the kids' bedroom first to kill them, taking the chance that Josiah or Sara Moore might wake up and come at him from behind."

That makes eminent sense to me. The Villisca Axe Murderer was deranged and depraved, yes, but that doesn't necessarily mean that he was *stupid*.

"I think he killed J.B. Moore first, and then killed Sara immediately afterward," Troy continues. "That's also based on the way that some of Sara's blood ended up on an article of his clothing. Then he killed the kids, in no particular order. My suspicion is that the Stillinger girls were killed last. I don't think the killer even knew that they were in the house..."

Had the murderer not been present at the church that night, or been watching the Moore residence from a hidden location, there's no way he could have known that Lena and Ina were accompanying the Moores back home, much less that they were occupying Katherine's bedroom for the night.

"Just as he did in the other Midwest Axe Murders, I think he cleaned up and went into the kitchen to make something to eat... he left behind an unfinished sandwich. My theory is that he heard a noise from the guest room, realized that the Moores were not the only people in the house. That's when he killed the Stillinger girls and then left."

Lena Stillinger's underwear had been removed, and her body was posed post mortem, with her genitalia exposed. Troy believes that this wasn't something done by the killer, but rather, that a second party came into the house *after* the murders had taken place. Who was this mysterious individual? None other than the Reverend George Kelly.

Troy's theory is that the perverted priest was out window-peeping, and happened to stumble upon the crime scene by chance. He then came into the house and staged the body of Lena Stillinger for his own perverse reasons. Kelly certainly had the opportunity to do so; he was the sole occupant of a house owned by Reverend Ewing, who was sleeping in a tent outside on the night of the 9th/10th in an attempt to ease his respiratory symptoms. Kelly was also undeniably a sexual deviant and a Peeping Tom. But I can't help but wonder how he could have seen what Troy believes he saw, given that the killer closed all of the curtains and covered the windows. He would have to have seen a stranger enter and then leave the Moore house early in the morning, carrying an axe with him; surmised what had just happened; and then, overcome with curiosity, entered the house in order to see for himself.

"Kelly knew a great deal about the crime scene itself," Troy explains, "and I think that's because he actually saw it for himself. He didn't kill anybody, but he was there after someone else did."

It's not beyond the realm of possibility, though my personal opinion remains that the killing of all eight occupants of the house, and the subsequent abuse of Lena Stillinger, was carried out by the same individual. Still, we will never know for sure, and Troy does make a compelling case. He's also the first to admit that it's just a theory, and he can't prove anything. Neither, for that matter, can I.

Why doesn't he find Kelly to be a credible suspect for the murders?

"This was a *tiny* little man, one who could barely have swung an axe that heavy. If he had been successful, he would have been absolutely covered in blood, but there was no sign of it when he was spotted on the train out of Villisca later that morning. I just don't see him as having the strength to overpower J.B. and kill everybody.

"Once I started looking at all of these other similar crime

scenes, which are almost *identical* to a T, ranging from Colorado Springs all the way to Kansas...I just can't buy that Kelly was responsible," Troy concludes. On that, I agree with him one hundred percent. George Kelly was not, to the best of our knowledge, in any of those towns or cities at the time of the other axe murders, and the similarity they bear to the Villisca killings is uncannily close.

"There are just too many points in common between them for it to be a coincidence," he says, putting my own thoughts into words. We both see eye-to-eye on the likelihood of the Villisca Axe Murders having been committed by a lone drifter who came into town on the train, and left the same way.

Other than a brief mention of the paranormal aspects in Roy Marshall's *Villisca*, other books on the subject have tended to focus on the murders themselves. Troy's book is different in that it also discusses the haunting.

"I've had experiences inside that house that could best be described as *interesting,*" he tells me. "Some have definitely been unnerving. But I've never really felt as if there was anything *evil* there, and I've never felt that whatever lingers there is connected with the killer. If anything, it feels more like it has something to do with the tragedy of the victims."

"Do you think there's a degree of 'you get whatever it is you take in there with you?'" I ask. In other words, does an individual who enters the Villisca Axe Murder House expecting something terrifying and evil encounter exactly that, whereas another, perhaps anticipating a meeting with the spirits of the murder victims, experience something which appears to be more child-like and playful?

"That does make sense," he agrees. "I hear from people that are reliable and credible, stories of truly frightening experiences they've had. I've never really been frightened in that house. I wouldn't say what's happened to me has been positive, exactly...if anything, it's been quite sad. There may well be all kinds of different energies in that house, and I think they could be attracting specific types of it to them, based upon their expectations."

Another possibility that I raise with Troy, is that of visitors like he and I ("ghost people," as I very affectionately call us) bringing along some kind of attachment from the numerous other haunted locations we visit. The idea isn't nearly as far-fetched as it sounds. Some people spend their vacation time sitting on a beach, hiking, rafting, or taking a cruise. We go to places such as Waverly Hills Sanatorium, The Stanley Hotel, The Bell Witch Cave...and then Villisca. Paranormal enthusiasts coming to Iowa often make the rounds of "the circuit," which includes Malvern Manor,

Farrar Elementary, Edinburgh Manor, and of course, the Villisca Axe Murder House. Could it be that entities are being unwittingly transported from location to location along with the paranormal enthusiasts, in the same way that we sometimes go to visit a friend's home and inadvertently track mud onto their carpet?

"That's definitely possible," Troy nods. "I always say that as I writer, I go into these places with the intention of telling their story, but sometimes you become a part of that story, whether you want to or not, and sometimes you take that story home with you...or perhaps even take it somewhere else."

Several mediums have said that there are numerous spirits both inside and around the house, which may well be explained away by how heavily-trafficked it is by paranormal investigators.

One of the most compelling accounts in Troy's book was his experience of the closet door opening and closing itself in the Moore children's bedroom.

"That was *weird*," he laughs. "It was my very first visit to the house. I was there with a group out of Nebraska named PRISM, and my friend, Anney Horn. Anney had told me that she thought Paul Moore was there in the bedroom with them, and that if we offered him candy, he would interact with us.

"Now, I wasn't there when it started opening and closing

itself on cue. I was downstairs, watching it on a video screen. The room was covered by a camera. I'm skeptical by nature, so at first, I thought this was just a bit of fun. Finally, I decided I had to go on up to the bedroom and see it for myself." He pauses for a moment, before going on. "We emptied out the entire house of people, then went through the place from top to bottom. We checked every single window and door, making sure that there were no drafts, nothing in the way of air movement or negative pressure that might explain it. There was no explanation whatsoever for what we'd seen.

"We left the camera covering that closet door for over an hour. It never moved an inch. Then Anney came back in the room and asked for the door to begin opening and closing again...*and it did*. It performed on command. I'd never seen anything like it. I'm not sure I *still* have, and I still can't give you a rational explanation for it."

Coming from a writer of Troy's reputation, this is very credible eyewitness testimony.

"I've had other things happen there that were similar, and they usually seem to involve the kids. I remember rolling a ball back and forth across the floor and watching it come to a complete stop, and then change direction, reversing course. Villisca is the only place I've ever seen that happen. I've tried to replicate that at other haunted locations — trigger objects hold a huge fascination for me

— but I've never been able to. It was the weirdest thing."

It might have been the weirdest thing to happen to Troy at Villisca, but it was far from the only thing. On one occasion, when he was in the house completely alone, he heard the unmistakable sound of footsteps following him from room to room, and then all the way up the staircase to the second floor. Doors also opened and closed themselves several times.

Troy has slept in the house a couple of times, breaking out a sleeping bag and crashing out on the floor of the parlor. Nothing disturbed him during the night.

"The first time I slept there by myself, I was pretty keyed up," he admits. "But I wasn't bothered by any uninvited visitors or woken up in the night."

Troy's comments about the paranormal activity he experienced at Villisca seeming to be connected with the victims, is a subject I want to explore further. I ask him what he thinks the likelihood is of something in the house *impersonating* the victims, rather than being a reflection of the victims themselves. He invokes the principal of Ockham's Razor: the concept that, given two competing theories, generally the simpler of the two tends to be the correct one.

"I've just always assumed that it was the victims," he reflects, though adding the caveat that he's "about as psychic as a doorknob." This is purely his instinct, he cautions me, and adds that I should take that for whatever it's worth. "I've never felt that what I've been interacting with was an adult. It always seemed childlike."

I find myself hoping that he's wrong about that, if only because it implies that the spirits of those children have been at the scene of their death for over a century, without even having the benefit of their parents to watch over them. I find the idea of a negative entity of some kind far more palatable, which tells me that I need to check my personal biases at the door when I investigate the house in person.

"Those spirits seem to be more interactive with adults that have kids," Troy observes. "As I said, I've never felt fearful or afraid around them. If anything, I've felt welcome, in fact. Accepted. Being a parent myself, perhaps I'm seen as a father figure of some kind, or at least somebody who's very comfortable around kids.

"What fascinates me most about Villisca is not just the killer and the murders, but the Moore family themselves, along with the Stillinger children." Troy immersed himself in every historical detail while he was writing his book, poring over newspaper articles and legal documents from those days. I don't have paranormal encounters that often, but Villisca is the exception. Every single time I've gone back to that house, something odd has happened. I can't say that about any other location."

Speaking of fascination, I ask Troy what he thinks is the

reason for the American public's enduring fascination with the Villisca Axe Murders. "There's the tragedy of seeing an entire family wiped out overnight," he muses, "and coupled with that is the fact that it's an eternal mystery. People love to speculate but we're never going to know for sure who did this. Because the house looks almost the same now as it did on the night of the murders, it's one of those rare places where you can walk the actual ground and connect with it on a personal level."

Our interview is coming to an end. I ask Troy whether there is any final message he would like to leave me with concerning the Villisca Axe Murder House. He pauses for a moment, giving the matter some thought.

"The one thing I always hope when people remember when they visit Villisca," Troy begins, "is that, while it's a really cool haunted location with a fascinating story, *eight people* were murdered in this house. Six of them were children. I try to impress on people to be aware of that, and be respectful of it, when they visit.

"I hope that people don't go to the Moore House and act like yahoos. I'm very fond of Villisca, and if you go there to experience it for yourself, please remember to be respectful...because respect is *everything*."

CHAPTER SIXTEEN
Making Sense of it All.

My involvement with the Villisca Axe Murder House haunting has so far spanned several years and multiple visits. I was always sufficiently intrigued by the place to want to go back and explore it further. It felt as if something was somehow drawing me back there, that I had unfinished business with the house.

I'm not claiming that this was anything paranormal, necessarily: it's more likely that the tragic tale of the Moore family and their young house guests, the Stillinger sisters, just resonated with me on a personal level. While it's true that everybody is fascinated with an unsolved mystery, as author Troy Taylor points out, there's also a lot more to it than that. Something about this unique residence speaks of a story needing to be told, or perhaps more accurately, of one that should be kept alive and relevant amidst the hustle and bustle of 21st century America. It speaks of simpler days, of a more innocent time — or at least, that's how we tend to perceive them now, although historians might argue differently.

Stepping inside the Moore residence today really does

feel like taking a step back in time, to the early days of the 20th century.

Many of the eyewitnesses that I interviewed during the course of researching this book, told of feeling a similar sort of attraction to the place, and to whatever it is that haunts it. Despite the horrific reason for the house's notoriety, it can be a peaceful and calm place to spend the evening...*if* the circumstances are right. More often, however, the atmosphere is uneasy and oppressive, as though the weight of the atrocity still casts a long shadow over the house to this day.

Johnny Houser, who is the undisputed expert on this particular case, has spent more than an entire year's worth of cumulative days and nights investigating the haunting. He has been inside the house on several anniversaries of the murders, during every different phase of the moon, in the summer, winter, spring and fall. He has investigated it on baking hot days when the temperature soared into the triple digits, and in the depths of winter, in sub-zero cold. Johnny also keeps a close eye on the many experiences that are being reported by visitors, whether they spend just an hour inside the house while taking a tour, or stay to investigate the property overnight.

It therefore stands to reason that, if anybody is in a position to spot a pattern arising amongst the paranormal activity reported at the house, Johnny Houser would be the man. Yet the fact remains that he has been unable to identify any rhyme or reason associated with the strange occurrences taking place at the Villisca Axe Murder House.

There are several schools of thought as to what, exactly, is behind the haunting. Of these, four seem to be the most popular, and bear further consideration.

Firstly, we have the opinion of people such as Troy Taylor, and medium Amy Allan, who believe that the spirits of the victims still linger inside the house. This is arguably the most disturbing explanation, as it means that anywhere up to eight spirits are stuck inside the house — which is also the scene of their own murder — because of an act of violence that was completely beyond their control.

A number of visiting mediums claim to have attempted to "cross over" the spirits of the victims, but whether this has actually taken place — or whether there was even anybody there to cross over in the first place — is unclear. Certainly, *something* inside the house likes to behave as if it is a child, or children (plural). I recorded the sound of a childlike giggle, and my colleagues also captured the sound of a child talking to itself.

The Klinge Brothers, Zak Bagans, Amy Bruni, Adam Berry, and other visitors have posited that the killer himself, or some kind of energy associated with him, is active at the house. The string of energy spikes that Brad and Barry Klinge's team recorded, moving in sequence from bed to bed and then out into the hallway, provides a fascinating piece of evidence to support this theory. Many of the more violent events which have taken place inside the house are attributed to the presence of the killer's spirit. While it is possible that this is the case, I find it to be one of the less likely possible explanations, not least because there is no evidence that the killer ever returned to the house during his lifetime after carrying out the murders. On the other hand, there are instances on record of killers such as Herb Baumeister and John Wayne Gacy supposedly haunting places they lived at or were familiar with during their lifetime, or objects that were associated with them.

Theory number three holds that there is a non-human entity — some people use the word *demonic* — at Villisca, either drawn there because of the negative energy generated by the murders, or perhaps unwittingly summoned to the house by one of the thousands of people who have visited since the renovation. This is certainly possible, although your perspective on this will depend on whether you believe in the existence of such entities or not. Seth Alne and his brother Jesse certainly do, and are convinced that the creature Jesse encountered in the house was just such an entity. Its motives, Jesse is convinced, were pure evil.

The fourth and final theory is the one proposed by Johnny Houser: that the Villisca Axe Murder House is actually haunting itself. This is the Thought Form hypothesis, the idea that an entity has somehow been paranormally created out of the many energies and thoughts which have passed through the property in the last 108 years...and perhaps, if people such as Dawn Biery are correct, even before then. One is forced to wonder whether there is more going on in this particular part of Villisca — or *Waliska/Wallisca*, whose meaning is 'evil spirit' — than first meets the eye.

Thousands of people entering the house and barn, all of them thinking about the murders of June 1912. All of them aware of the ghost stories told by tour guides, fueled by TV shows and media accounts, even books such as this one; we are forced to ask whether this all feeds such a Thought Form, strengthens it, and allows it to grow. That's a lot of potential energy, much of it negative, and a very powerful fuel source if it can be tapped into by something capable of doing so.

Perhaps we, the readers, the viewers, and the visitors alike, are all partly responsible for helping the Villisca Axe Murder House haunt itself.

Sleep well.

Richard Estep
Longmont,
Colorado
August 20, 2020

Acknowledgments

Firstly, to you, the reader: Thank you for spending your hard-earned money and valuable time in order to read this book. It is my sincere hope that you have enjoyed it, and would ask you to please consider rating the book on Amazon's website. In the current writing market, books tend to live and die by their reviews and ratings, particularly on Amazon. Your help would therefore be greatly appreciated.

The author would like to extend his sincerest thanks to the following people, without whom this book would not have been possible.

Johnny Houser

Troy Taylor

Martha Linn

Stephen Weidner

Erik Bensen

Dawn Biery

Seth and Jesse Alne

Chris Dedman

Sarah Stream

Catlyn Keenan

Jason and Linda Fellon

Charlie Stiffler (and Stiffler's Mom)

Last, but by no means least, thanks to Laura, for her unflinching support.

Much love to you all,
Richard
If you feel so inclined, please visit me over at my web page, **www.richardestep.net.** I love to hear from readers, so drop by and say hi!

Printed in Great Britain
by Amazon